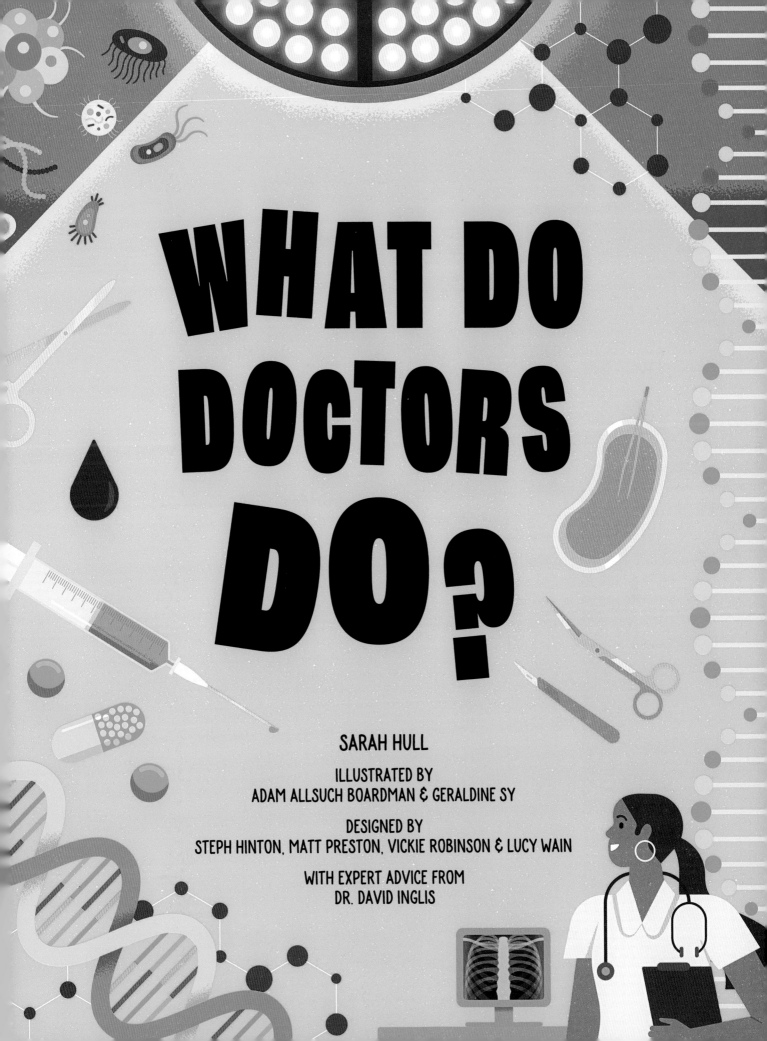

WHAT DO DOCTORS DO?

SARAH HULL

ILLUSTRATED BY
ADAM ALLSUCH BOARDMAN & GERALDINE SY

DESIGNED BY
STEPH HINTON, MATT PRESTON, VICKIE ROBINSON & LUCY WAIN

WITH EXPERT ADVICE FROM
DR. DAVID INGLIS

Usborne Quicklinks

For links to websites where you can watch doctors at work, see inside the human body and find out more about how doctors help their patients, go to **usborne.com/Quicklinks** and type in the title of this book.

Here are some things you can do at the sites we recommend:
- Watch air ambulance doctors in action.
- Meet a robot that helps a doctor in the operating room.
- Take a virtual tour of a children's hospital.

Children should be supervised online.
Please follow the internet safety guidelines at
Usborne Quicklinks. Usborne is not responsible for
the content or availability of external websites.

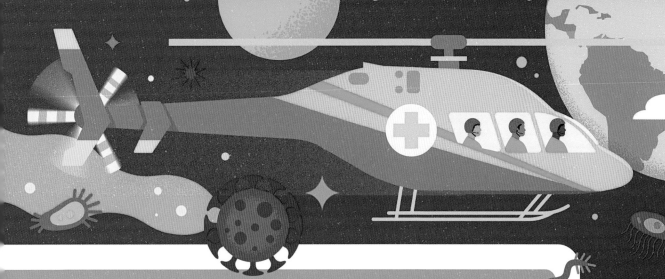

Contents

What do doctors do? 4

Disease detectives 6

Working in a busy hospital 16

Emergency! 26

Life-saving surgery 36

Keeping everyone healthy 46

Fascinating brains 54

The future of medicine 62

How to become a doctor 68

You can check
the meaning of any
medical words you don't
know on pages 76–77.

WHAT DO DOCTORS DO?

Lots of people are called doctors, but not all of them could help if you got sick.

Sometimes "doctor" just means someone has studied to a high level at university. Only a MEDICAL DOCTOR can diagnose and treat medical problems.

Becoming a medical doctor takes huge skill – years studying medicine at university, followed by years of training on the job. It's hard work, but also very rewarding.

How do doctors work out what's happening INSIDE someone's body?

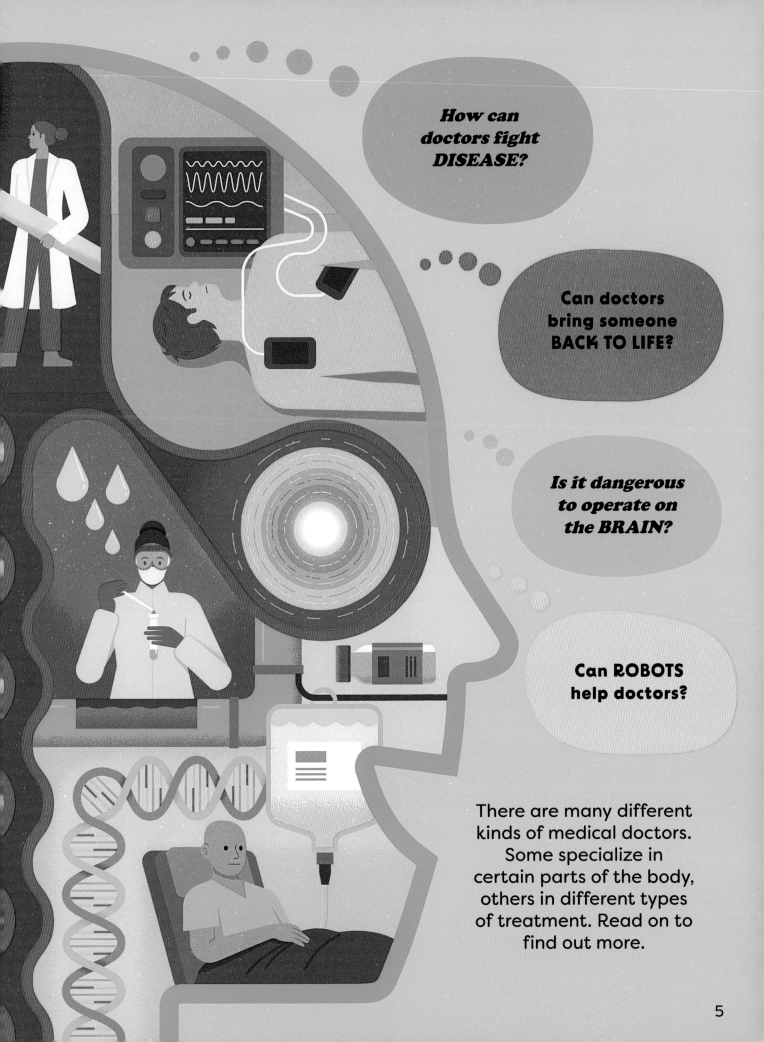

There are many different kinds of medical doctors. Some specialize in certain parts of the body, others in different types of treatment. Read on to find out more.

Disease detectives

Like detectives, doctors have to hunt for clues when someone has a medical problem, and puzzle out what they mean. This is called **diagnosis** and it's especially important for these jobs...

PRIMARY CARE PHYSICIANS (PCPs) are usually the first doctors you see when you feel sick. They work in a doctor's office, looking after people who live locally. They may also be called **FAMILY PHYSICIANS**, **GENERAL PRACTITIONERS (GPs)** or **INTERNISTS**.

RADIOLOGISTS look at X-rays and other images that show inside the body, to see what's going on. They usually work in hospitals.

PATHOLOGISTS work in labs, where they examine urine and other samples from patients, for signs of disease.

HEMATOLOGISTS are blood specialists. They do a lot of work in labs, analyzing blood samples.

Meeting patients

PRIMARY CARE PHYSICIANS are usually the first disease detectives a patient meets. These patient-doctor meetings are called **consultations**.

A typical day might start like this...

Primary care physicians may talk to many different patients in a day. They have to know all about common medical problems, including mental health.

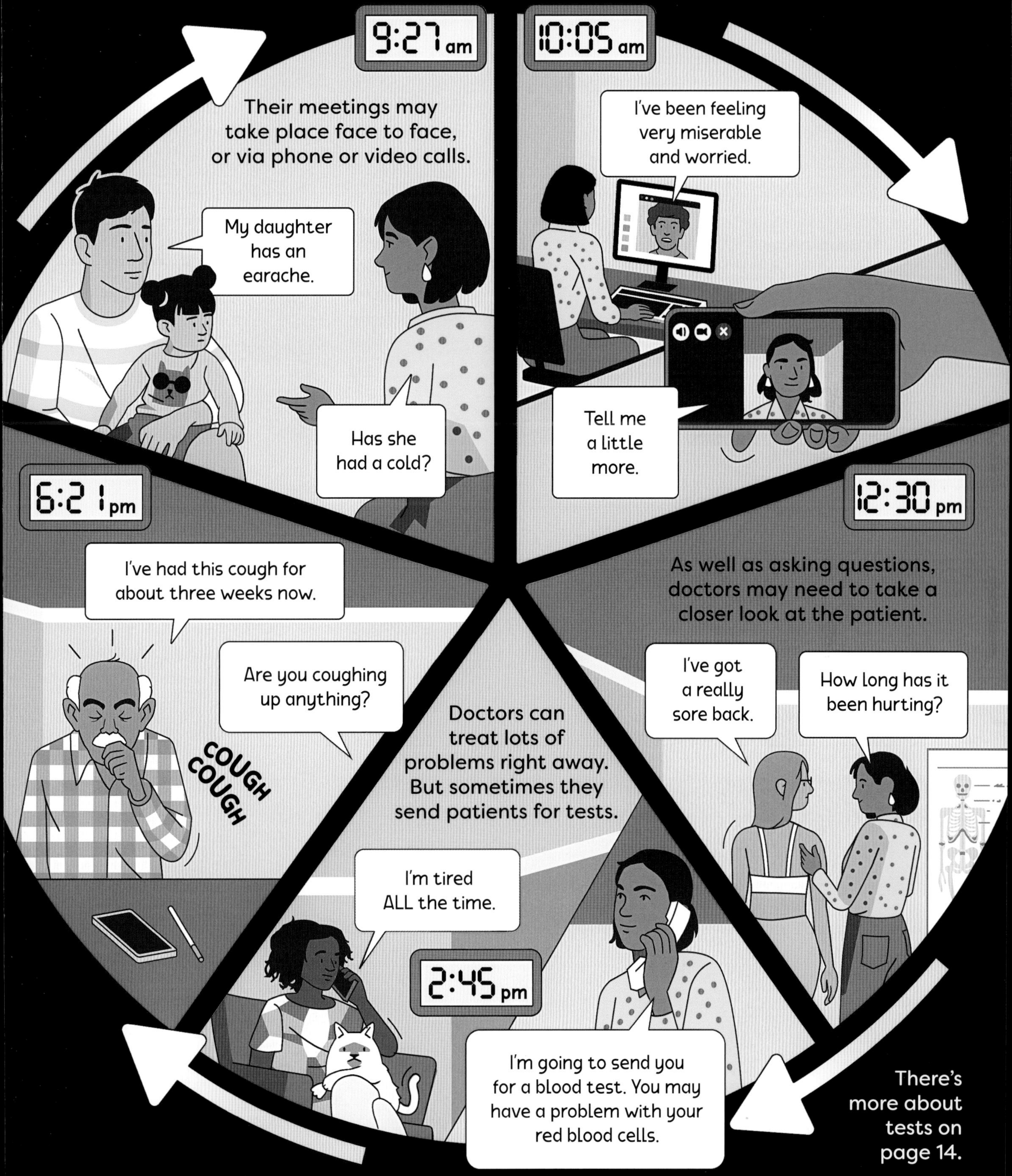

There's more about tests on page 14.

Vital signs

To check your health, doctors measure lots of things in your body. The ones below are known as vital signs.

PULSE

This is how fast the heart is pumping blood around the body.

A healthy adult's heart will beat about **60–100 times a minute.**

To take someone's pulse, the doctor presses two fingers into their wrist.

Then they count how many "thwumps" they feel in a minute.

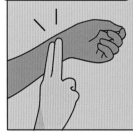

If the pulse is too fast or slow, the heart may be struggling.

BODY TEMPERATURE

This is how hot or cold someone is.

Body temperature varies, but is normally around **36.5–37.5°C (97.7–99.5°F).**

A high temperature, or fever, can be a sign of an infection.

Ear thermometer

If body temperature rises or falls by even one degree, the brain and other organs may start to struggle.

BREATHING RATE

This is how fast someone is breathing.

A healthy adult usually takes around **12–16 breaths per minute.**

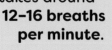

We breathe to take in oxygen in the air. If someone is breathing too fast or too slow, they may not be taking in enough.

BLOOD PRESSURE

This is how hard blood pushes as it races around the body.

It's measured in units called millimeters of mercury (mmHg), because early gauges to test it contained mercury.

A healthy adult level is between **90/60** and **120/80 mmHg.**

A squeezy armband is used to measure it.

Left untreated, high blood pressure can lead to heart attacks and other problems.

Blood pressure monitor

148
92

Physical examinations

When a doctor looks at, feels or listens to parts of someone's body, it's called a **physical examination.**

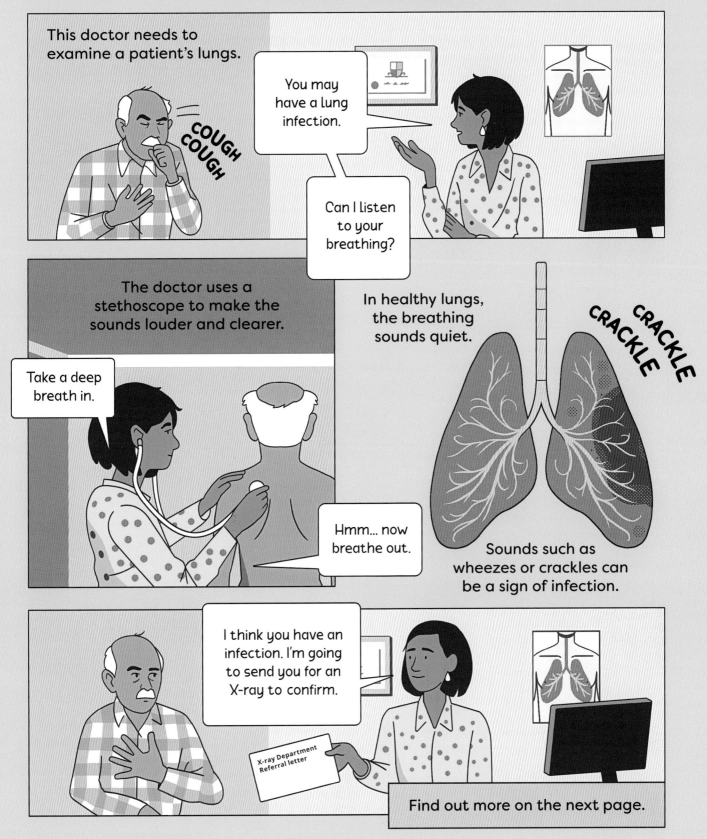

Find out more on the next page.

Seeing inside

Sometimes, doctors need to see what's going on **inside** a patient's body to figure out what's wrong. They have several ways to do this.

X-rays

An X-ray machine sends out X-rays – powerful waves of energy that you can't see. The X-rays pass through your body, but not through your bones. The machine detects where the X-rays get through to make an image.

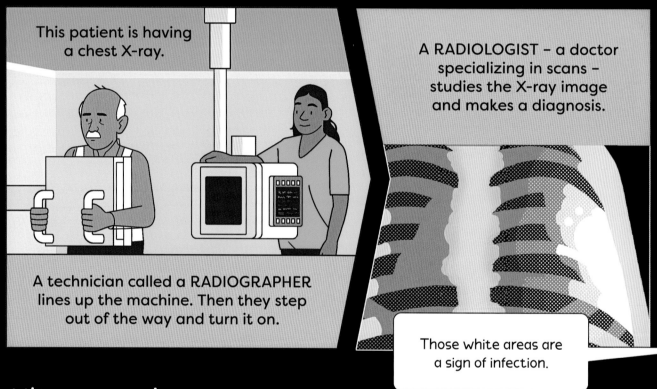

This patient is having a chest X-ray.

A technician called a RADIOGRAPHER lines up the machine. Then they step out of the way and turn it on.

A RADIOLOGIST – a doctor specializing in scans – studies the X-ray image and makes a diagnosis.

Those white areas are a sign of infection.

Ultrasound

Some scanners use ultrasound (sounds too high to hear) to make images.

The sound passes through some parts of the body and bounces off others, creating echoes – which the scanner detects.

Ultrasound scans can show babies before they are born.

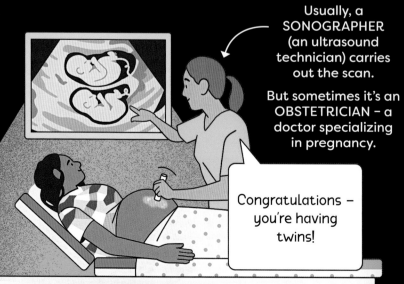

Usually, a SONOGRAPHER (an ultrasound technician) carries out the scan.

But sometimes it's an OBSTETRICIAN – a doctor specializing in pregnancy.

Congratulations – you're having twins!

More detail

CT and MRI scanners allow doctors to see detailed slice-by-slice images of the body.
CT (Computed Tomography) scanners do this with X-rays, while MRI (Magnetic Resonance Imaging) scanners use strong magnets.

This patient is having a CT scan after hitting his head, to check for bleeding in the brain.

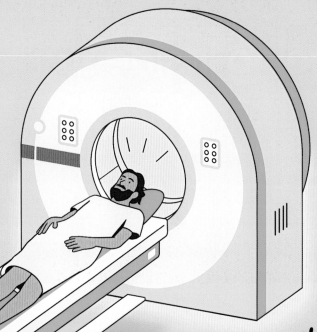

CLANK CLANK
WHIRRRRRRRR

A radiologist studies the images. She has to work fast, because bleeding in the brain (if there is any) needs to be treated quickly.

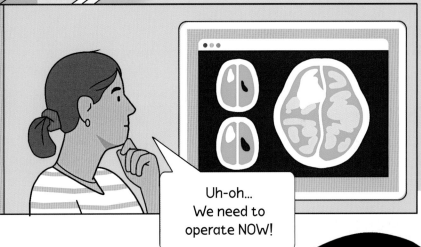

Uh-oh...
We need to operate NOW!

Radioactive scans

For some scans, a technician or nurse injects a radioactive substance into the body. The substance gives off radioactive rays.

The rays are picked up by a scanner. So, doctors can watch where the substance goes and see if it reveals a problem.

Fluorodeoxyglucose

Being a radiologist means working with incredibly advanced technology – and new scanners and techniques are always appearing.

13

Tests and samples

Another way to look for clues is to take a **sample** – a little bit of something from a patient – and test it. Testing is the job of doctors called PATHOLOGISTS and HEMATOLOGISTS.

Hematologists zoom in on blood with a microscope to reveal important clues.

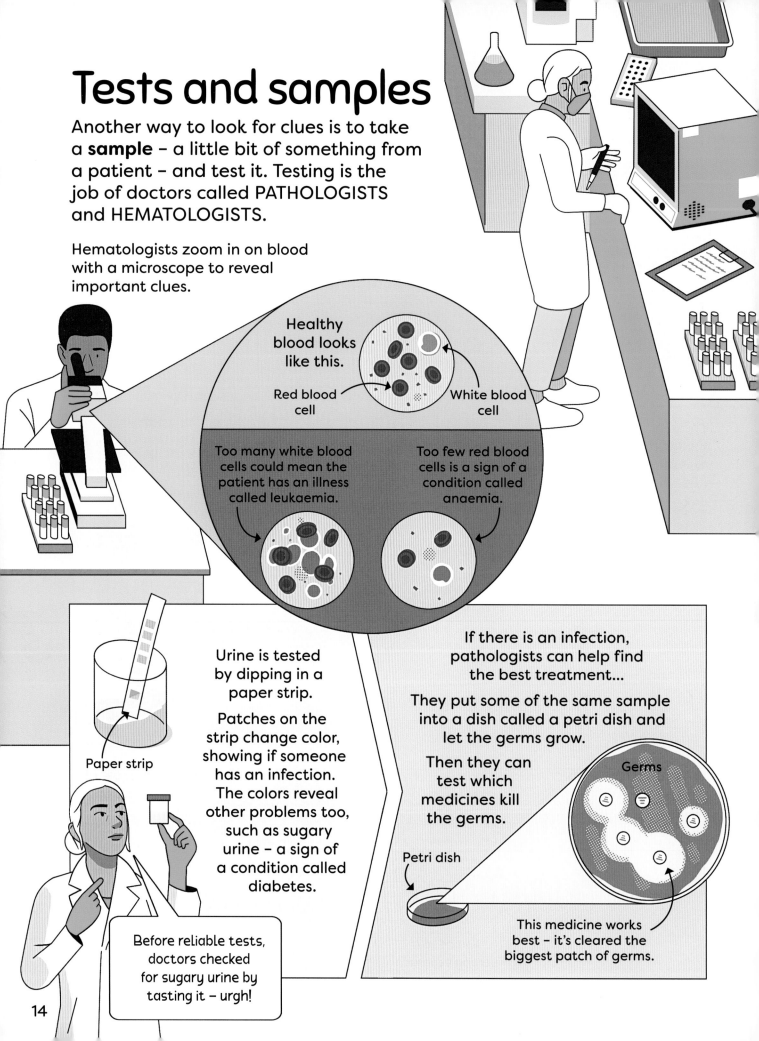

Healthy blood looks like this.

Red blood cell

White blood cell

Too many white blood cells could mean the patient has an illness called leukaemia.

Too few red blood cells is a sign of a condition called anaemia.

Paper strip

Urine is tested by dipping in a paper strip.

Patches on the strip change color, showing if someone has an infection. The colors reveal other problems too, such as sugary urine – a sign of a condition called diabetes.

Before reliable tests, doctors checked for sugary urine by tasting it – urgh!

If there is an infection, pathologists can help find the best treatment...

They put some of the same sample into a dish called a petri dish and let the germs grow.

Then they can test which medicines kill the germs.

Germs

Petri dish

This medicine works best – it's cleared the biggest patch of germs.

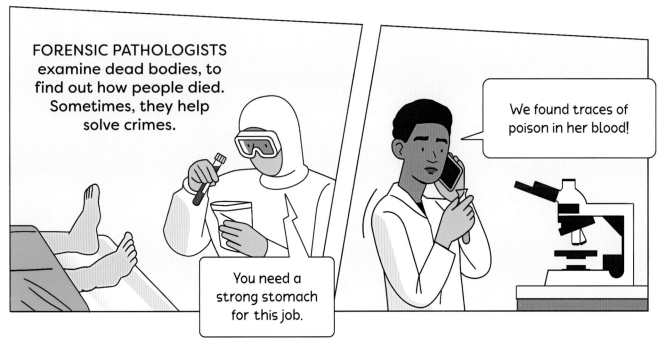

Working in a busy hospital

You'll find more different kinds of doctors in a hospital than anywhere else. Here are just a few of them.

PEDIATRICIANS are doctors who look after sick children.

NEONATOLOGISTS are doctors who look after newborn babies, especially ones that are unwell or born early.

OBSTETRICIANS provide care during pregnancy and birth.

DERMATOLOGISTS diagnose and treat skin problems.

GERIATRICIANS are experts in treating older people.

CODE RED

In the hospital

Welcome to the hospital! If you become a doctor, you'll spend at least a few years working here while you train – and possibly many more.

Many doctors see patients in parts of the hospital called **clinics**. These patients are **outpatients** who go home after their appointments.

In the dermatology clinic, a skin doctor, or DERMATOLOGIST, is seeing a patient.

OUTPATIENT CLINICS

← AUDIOLOGY

← PRENATAL CLINIC

← DERMATOLOGY

↱ GERIATRIC

→ CARDIOLOGY

My doctor thought I should get this mole checked.

Hmm... it's very irregular and bumpy. I think we should remove it and run some tests.

Follow the signs to AUDIOLOGY. It's on the third floor.

I've come for a hearing test.

← RADIOLOGY

← OPERATING THEATERS

← PATHOLOGY

Oooo...

RECEPTION

You can see inside an operating theater on pages 38–39.

Some doctors have patients who are too sick to go home. These patients are given a bed on a **ward**.

WARDS

L4	**GERIATRIC WARD**
L3	**NEONATAL INTENSIVE CARE UNIT**
L2	**PEDIATRIC WARD**
L2	**MATERNITY WARD**
L1	**GENERAL SURGICAL WARD**

You can find out about the jobs people do here on pages 24–25.

In the geriatric ward, a GERIATRICIAN – a doctor who works with older patients – is assessing a patient.

When you're better, I'll see you for check-ups in my clinic.

The hospital has around twice as many nurses as doctors. Like doctors, we see patients in clinics and look after them on wards.

NURSE

I'm Raj, a new doctor here.

SECURITY

Welcome to the team! You'll need this keycard to get around.

It takes **thousands** of people to run a hospital. As well as doctors and nurses, there are security, staff who move patients and equipment, pharmacists who keep medicine stores stocked, and many, many more.

Doing the rounds

On the wards, doctors start each day with a **ward round** – a visit to every patient in their care.

PEDIATRIC WARD

PEDIATRICIANS are doctors who look after children. These pediatricians are just starting their ward round. The team checks medication, looks at test results and decides the next steps.

9:03 am

How are you feeling?

Better, but still tired.

One doctor updates the patients' notes as they go.

9:16 am

The scan was all clear, so you'll be able to go home today.

Hurray!

9:28 am

This patient had a bad attack of asthma, a condition that affects the airways.

Once you're breathing more easily, a new inhaler should help keep the asthma under control.

9:38 am

This patient has a bad vomiting bug. As vomiting bugs spread easily, doctors wear protective clothes and keep the patient in a side room.

The tests we did show it was a bug called norovirus. He'll be better soon.

Night shift

At the end of a busy day, clinics close and outpatients and visitors leave. But for doctors on the night shift, work is just beginning.

Not all doctors work night shifts, but the ones with the sickest patients often do.

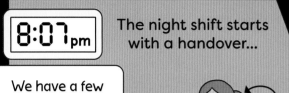

8:07pm The night shift starts with a handover...

We have a few complex patients...

Night doctor

Day doctor

OK, I'll make sure to see them first.

The night doctor picks up a pager – a device that vibrates when help is needed.

BRRRR

2460

The doctor phones the number on the screen to find out what's going on.

Please see the patient on bed 6, with low urine.

9:23pm

I'm going to put in a drip to give you fluid.

Tired brains are more likely to make mistakes. So at night, doctors only do jobs that can't wait until morning.

1:44am When things are quiet, doctors try to rest.

BRRRR

But if their pager goes off, they spring back into action.

Welcoming new babies

In some parts of the hospital, doctors work with other medical staff to help babies get the best start in life.

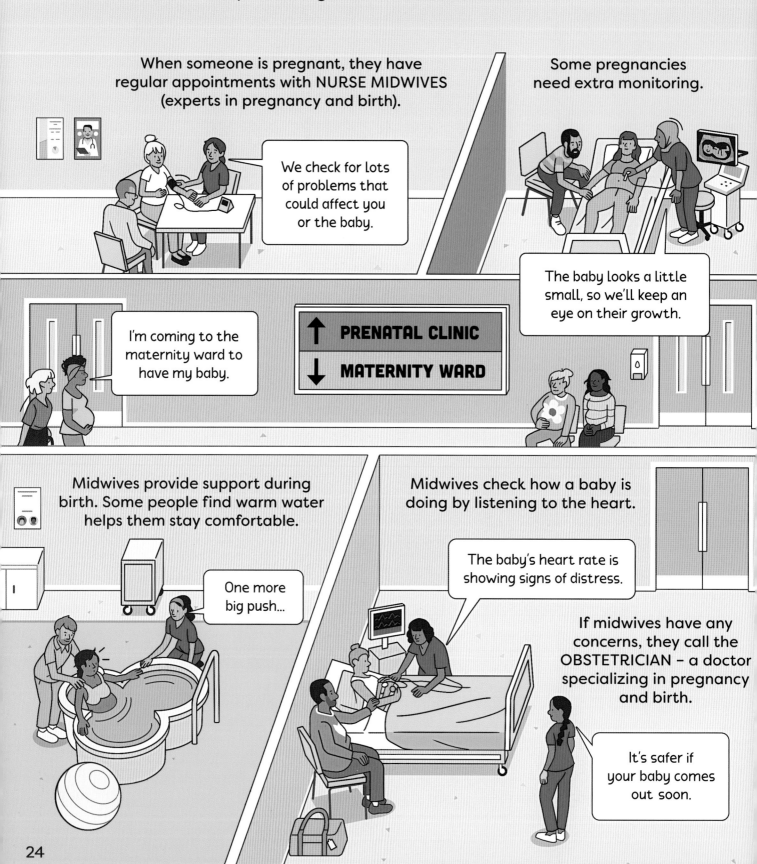

When someone is pregnant, they have regular appointments with NURSE MIDWIVES (experts in pregnancy and birth).

We check for lots of problems that could affect you or the baby.

Some pregnancies need extra monitoring.

The baby looks a little small, so we'll keep an eye on their growth.

I'm coming to the maternity ward to have my baby.

↑ PRENATAL CLINIC

↓ MATERNITY WARD

Midwives provide support during birth. Some people find warm water helps them stay comfortable.

One more big push...

Midwives check how a baby is doing by listening to the heart.

The baby's heart rate is showing signs of distress.

If midwives have any concerns, they call the OBSTETRICIAN – a doctor specializing in pregnancy and birth.

It's safer if your baby comes out soon.

Obstetricians can perform an operation, called a **cesarean section**, to get the baby out.

An ANESTHESIOLOGIST – a doctor who stops patients from feeling pain during surgery – gives an injection.

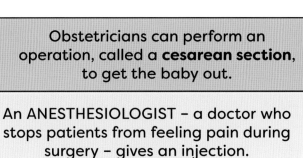

You won't feel anything from the chest down.

The obstetrician makes a cut in the abdomen.

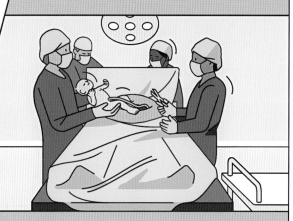

In an emergency, obstetricians can get the baby out in a matter of minutes.

Sometimes, a distressed baby passes meconium (a first poop) before it's born. This can cause problems if it gets into the baby's mouth or airway.

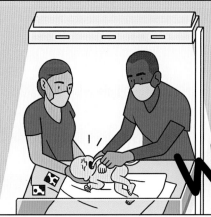

Doctors have to suck it away quickly, so the baby can take its first breath.

WAAAAHH

We'll keep your baby in the Neonatal Intensive Care Unit for a few days, until her lungs are stronger.

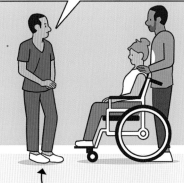

Doctors called NEONATOLOGISTS look after sick newborn babies.

NEONATAL INTENSIVE CARE UNIT

This is an **incubator**. It keeps the baby warm.

Goodbye! Thank you!

I love my job – it can be dramatic, but it's very joyful.

Emergency!

When there's a medical emergency, these doctors know exactly what to do.

EMERGENCY ROOM DOCTORS treat people with injuries and emergency medical conditions when they arrive at the hospital.

INTENSIVE CARE DOCTORS look after the sickest patients in hospital.

AIR AMBULANCE DOCTORS fly out to give urgent emergency care to patients on the spot.

HUMANITARIAN DOCTORS help out when disaster strikes, anywhere in the world.

EXPEDITION DOCTORS work in extreme locations, dealing with whatever medical problems arise.

The Emergency Room

When people are injured or suddenly get sick, they go to ER* – the hospital's department for emergencies and accidents. Here, specialist ER DOCTORS are on hand to help.

Work in the ER is fast-paced. There are lots of patients to see – and more arriving all the time.

Patients sign in, then wait to see a nurse. The nurse decides whether patients need to see a doctor, and who needs the most urgent care.

Aliyah Salem?

Coming!

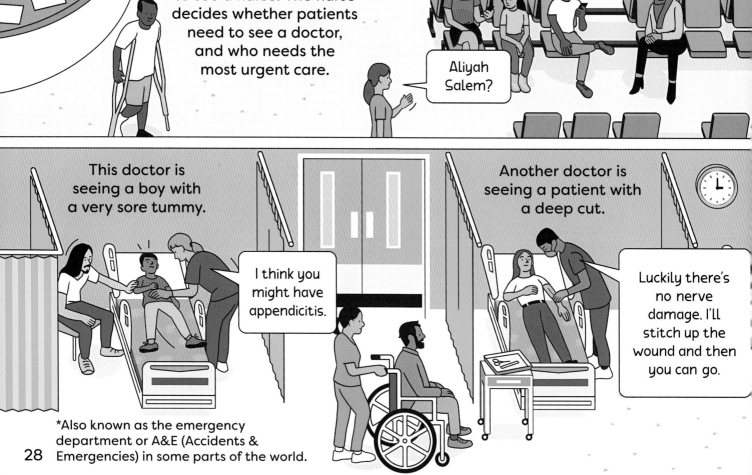

This doctor is seeing a boy with a very sore tummy.

I think you might have appendicitis.

Another doctor is seeing a patient with a deep cut.

Luckily there's no nerve damage. I'll stitch up the wound and then you can go.

*Also known as the emergency department or A&E (Accidents & Emergencies) in some parts of the world.

28

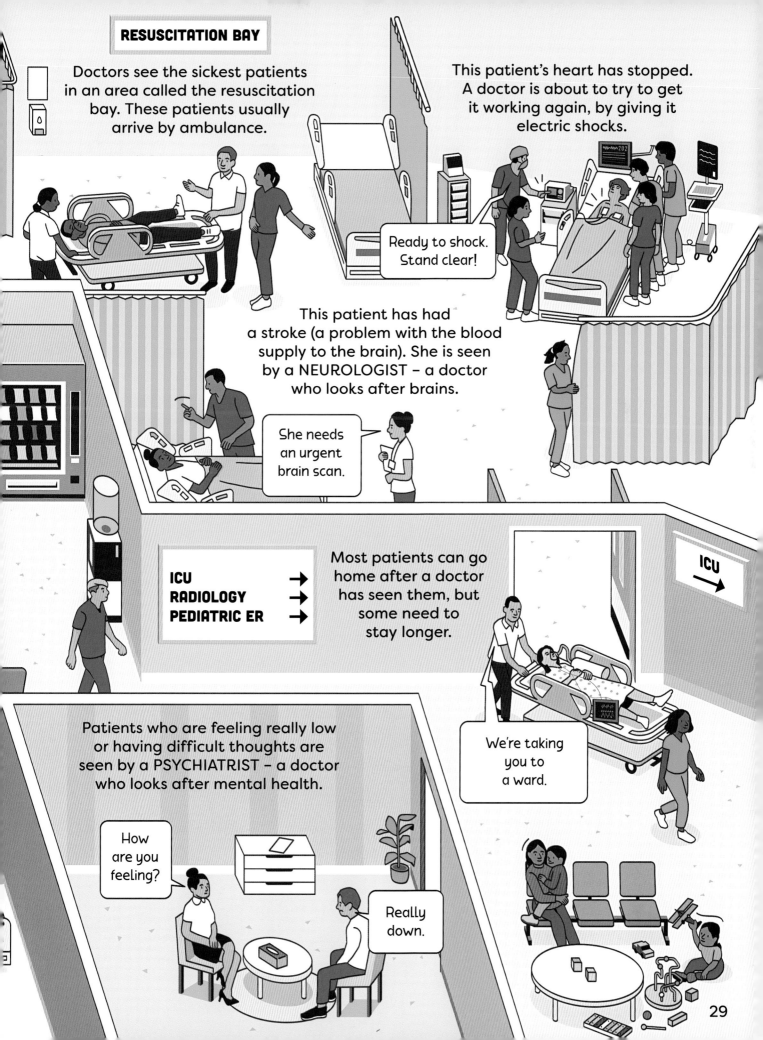

RESUSCITATION BAY

Doctors see the sickest patients in an area called the resuscitation bay. These patients usually arrive by ambulance.

This patient's heart has stopped. A doctor is about to try to get it working again, by giving it electric shocks.

Ready to shock. Stand clear!

This patient has had a stroke (a problem with the blood supply to the brain). She is seen by a NEUROLOGIST – a doctor who looks after brains.

She needs an urgent brain scan.

ICU   →
RADIOLOGY   →
PEDIATRIC ER →

Most patients can go home after a doctor has seen them, but some need to stay longer.

ICU →

We're taking you to a ward.

Patients who are feeling really low or having difficult thoughts are seen by a PSYCHIATRIST – a doctor who looks after mental health.

How are you feeling?

Really down.

29

Intensive care

The sickest hospital patients are kept in Intensive Care Units (ICU) – where they are looked after by a team of INTENSIVE CARE DOCTORS and nurses.

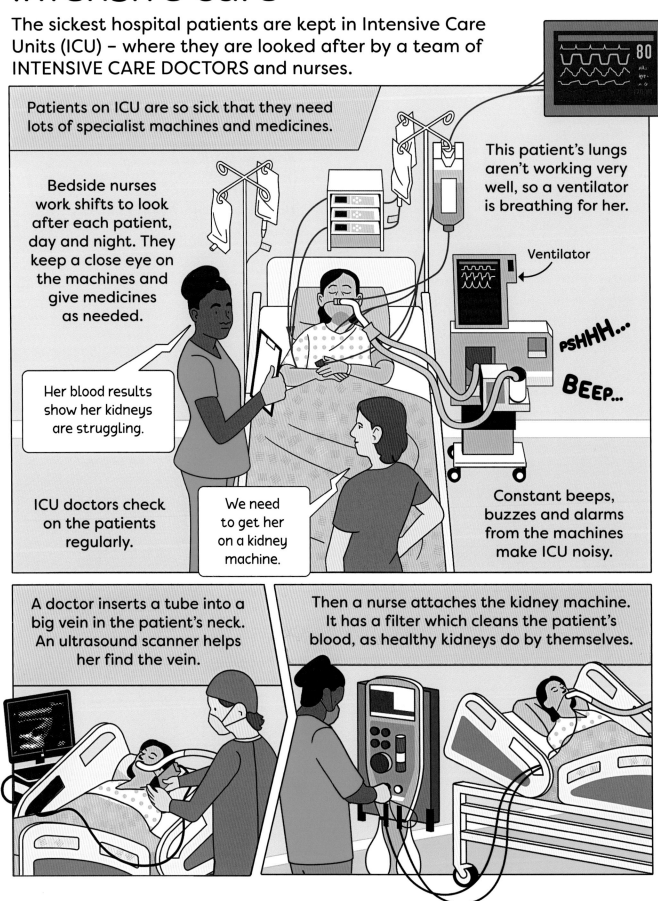

Patients on ICU are so sick that they need lots of specialist machines and medicines.

Bedside nurses work shifts to look after each patient, day and night. They keep a close eye on the machines and give medicines as needed.

Her blood results show her kidneys are struggling.

ICU doctors check on the patients regularly.

We need to get her on a kidney machine.

This patient's lungs aren't working very well, so a ventilator is breathing for her.

Ventilator

PSHHH...

BEEP...

Constant beeps, buzzes and alarms from the machines make ICU noisy.

A doctor inserts a tube into a big vein in the patient's neck. An ultrasound scanner helps her find the vein.

Then a nurse attaches the kidney machine. It has a filter which cleans the patient's blood, as healthy kidneys do by themselves.

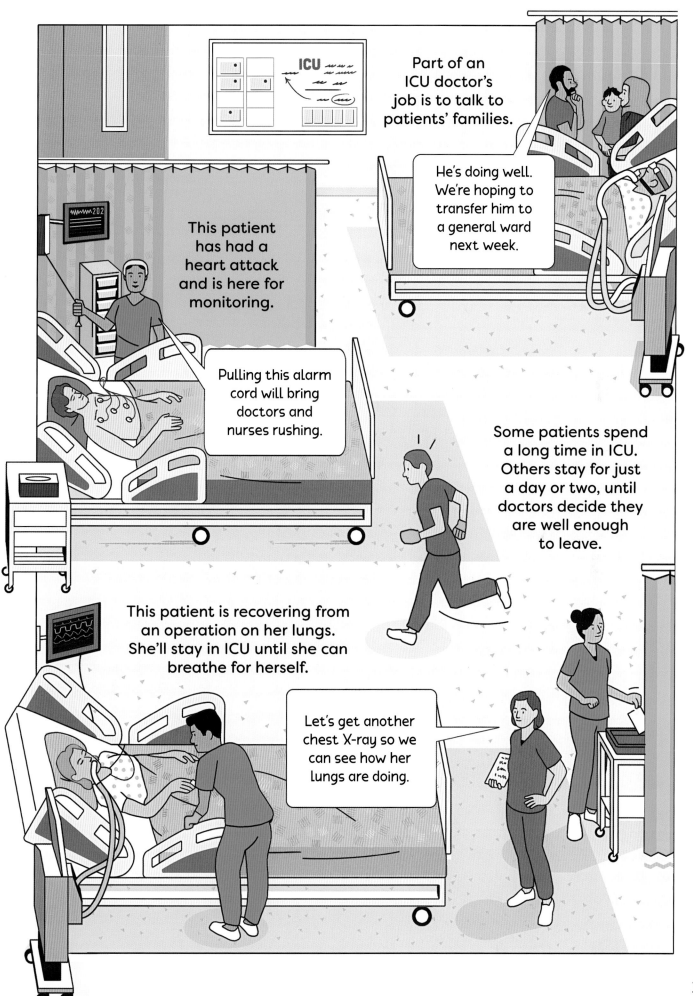

Help from the sky

When someone's badly hurt, AIR AMBULANCE DOCTORS can fly to wherever they are very quickly, and start emergency care right there and then.

This air ambulance doctor, paramedic, and pilot have been called out to a car crash in the countryside, far from the nearest hospital. The driver is badly wounded.

CHAKKA...
CHAAKK...

I think I can land there, on the grass.

Air ambulance doctors are trained to deal with all kinds of injuries.
On board the helicopter, they have everything they need...

Equipment to monitor a patient's heart and lungs

OXYGEN

Breathing equipment and mask

Emergency surgical kit

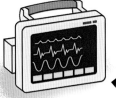
Cooler bags with supplies of blood

If a patient is bleeding a lot, giving them blood can keep them alive.

Defibrillator – this can restart a heart if a patient had a heart attack.

I can perform all kinds of emergency surgery – even heart surgery.

DOCTOR

At the scene, the doctor and paramedic quickly assess the patient and start treatment. With serious injuries, every second counts, and the team has to stay calm.

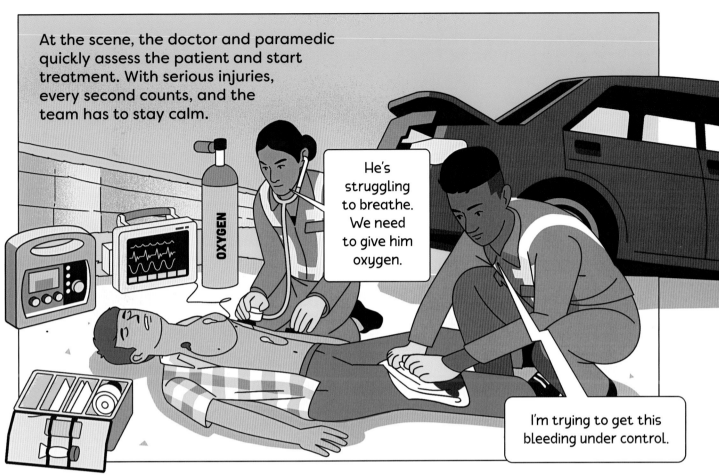

When the doctor decides the patient is stable, the air ambulance takes him to hospital for more treatment.

Back at base, it's time to debrief. That means talking through every detail of what happened.

Doctors and paramedics see lots of upsetting things, and it helps to talk about them. Debriefs also help the team learn from every mission.

Daring doctors

Some brave doctors choose to work in the most difficult places on Earth – from deadly war zones to the deep freeze of Antarctica.

Doctors doing **humanitarian work** provide extra medical care wherever it is most needed. That could be in the middle of a war, a crowded refugee camp, or a natural disaster.

Inflatable hospitals, like this one, can be put up in a matter of days.

Inside this tent, there's an operation taking place.

Next, please!

Do things look blurry?

Doctors and nurses here may have to deal with war wounds or dangerous diseases. They also help with everyday medical problems.

We need to get the baby out quickly.

Adventurers

EXPEDITION DOCTORS work in some of the most extraordinary places in the world. And sometimes the medical problems they deal with are extraordinary as well.

An expedition doctor must be able to treat any problem the team encounters. That could mean recognizing a rare tropical disease, or...

SNAKE BITE!

We've got to get back to camp – you need an antivenom injection!

This jungle has dozens of different venomous snakes. The doctor needs to know how to treat a bite from any of them.

Researchers in Antarctica are cut off from the rest of the world for eight months, during the bitterly cold winter. And there's just one doctor...

I have to deal with everything – from dentistry and depression, to major surgery.

Dr. Jerri Nielsen

Dr. Jerri Nielsen developed breast cancer while working here in 1999.

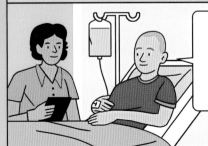

I had to operate on myself, and take strong anti-cancer drugs.

As soon as a plane could land, Dr. Nielsen was taken to hospital for more treatment – and recovered.

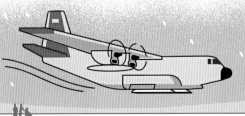

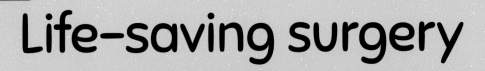

Life-saving surgery

Sometimes, the only way to fix a problem is to cut someone open. That's the job of doctors called surgeons.

GENERAL SURGEONS do common operations, such as removing a swollen appendix (a minor organ) or repairing a hole in muscle, known as a hernia.

ORTHOPEDIC SURGEONS repair broken bones and joints. They use saws and drills, so they're sometimes jokingly called carpenters.

OTOLARYNGOLOGISTS operate on ears, noses and throats. They are also known as **ENTs**.

CARDIOTHORACIC SURGEONS operate on hearts and lungs.

PLASTIC SURGEONS restore the appearance of parts of the body after disease or injury.

ANESTHESIOLOGISTS put patients to sleep before operations so they can't feel anything, and monitor them while surgeons work.

In the operating theater

Some operations are planned. Others are carried out in emergencies. Operations can take just a few minutes, or many hours. They take place in rooms called operating theaters.

Patients are more likely to get an infection if they have surgery. So, everything is kept as germ-free as possible.

Before operating, surgeons and nurses "scrub up." They clean their hands...

> We turn the faucets on and off with our elbows.

...and put on super-clean surgical gowns and gloves.

> The gowns and gloves are specially folded so we only touch the insides.

OPERATING THEATER ONE

This patient is having a planned operation to repair an injured knee. An orthopedic surgeon will replace the knee joint with a metal one – with help from the team.

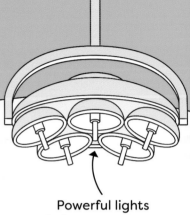

Powerful lights help surgeons see super clearly.

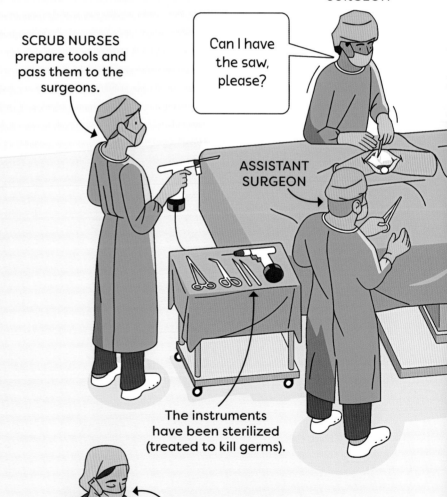

ORTHOPEDIC SURGEON

> Can I have the saw, please?

SCRUB NURSES prepare tools and pass them to the surgeons.

ASSISTANT SURGEON

The instruments have been sterilized (treated to kill germs).

THEATER ASSISTANTS check medicines and fetch supplies.

Most surgeons spend around half their time in the operating theater.

The rest of their time is spent updating patients' notes...

...assessing patients.

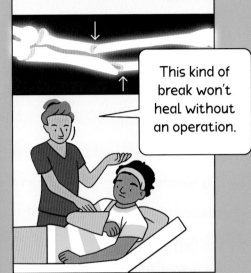

This kind of break won't heal without an operation.

ANESTHESIOLOGIST

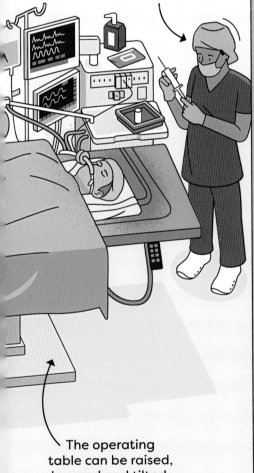
The operating table can be raised, lowered and tilted, so surgeons can work comfortably.

...explaining risks.

One leg may end up a tiny bit shorter.

...checking how patients are recovering.

Staying active will help you heal.

...and preparing for tricky operations.

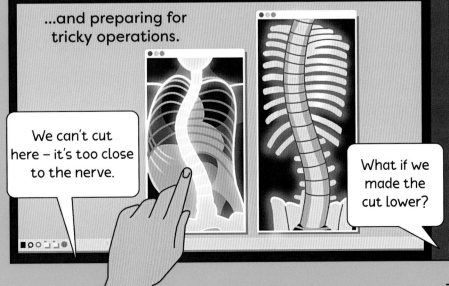

We can't cut here – it's too close to the nerve.

What if we made the cut lower?

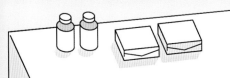

Performing surgery

Surgeons use an incredible range of techniques and equipment, depending on the operation. Here are some of them...

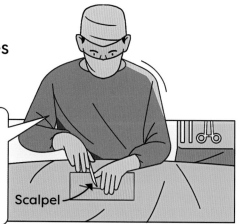

OPEN SURGERY

This means using a sharp blade called a scalpel to cut into the problem area.

> I'm going to remove a growth from this patient's stomach.

Scalpel

LONDON, UNITED KINGDOM

ROBOTIC SURGERY

Using a computer to control robot arms allows surgeons to make very precise movements, and view them all on a screen.

Usually, with robotic surgery, the surgeon is in the same room as the patient. But surgeons can operate from another hospital – even one on the other side of the world.

> Before operating on patients, I spent hours perfecting each movement on a practice robot that uses virtual reality.

Surgeon

BOGOTA, COLOMBIA

A camera shows the surgeon what's going on inside the body.

Image from camera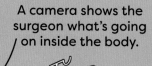

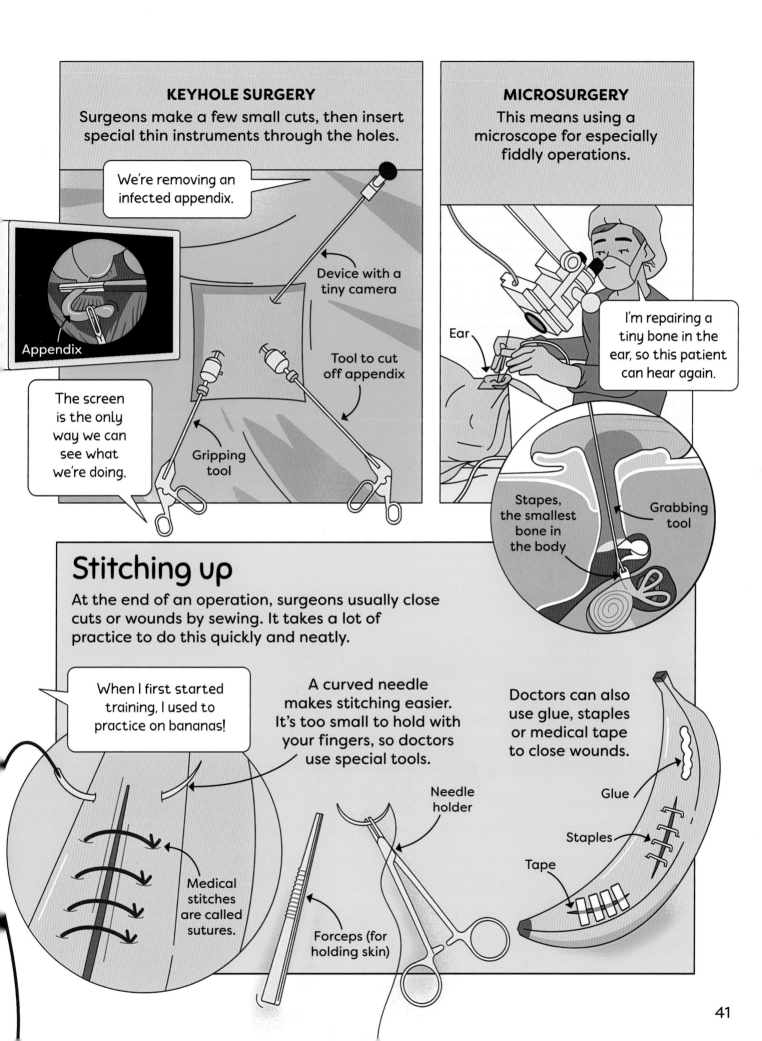

KEYHOLE SURGERY
Surgeons make a few small cuts, then insert special thin instruments through the holes.

We're removing an infected appendix.

Appendix

Device with a tiny camera

The screen is the only way we can see what we're doing.

Tool to cut off appendix

Gripping tool

MICROSURGERY
This means using a microscope for especially fiddly operations.

I'm repairing a tiny bone in the ear, so this patient can hear again.

Ear

Stapes, the smallest bone in the body

Grabbing tool

Stitching up
At the end of an operation, surgeons usually close cuts or wounds by sewing. It takes a lot of practice to do this quickly and neatly.

When I first started training, I used to practice on bananas!

A curved needle makes stitching easier. It's too small to hold with your fingers, so doctors use special tools.

Doctors can also use glue, staples or medical tape to close wounds.

Medical stitches are called sutures.

Needle holder

Glue

Staples

Tape

Forceps (for holding skin)

Pain-free surgery

Most surgery would be impossible without ANESTHESIOLOGISTS. These doctors put the patient to sleep for the operation, and make sure they don't feel pain.

Before an operation, the anesthesiologist gives the patient a mix of drugs to make them sleep.

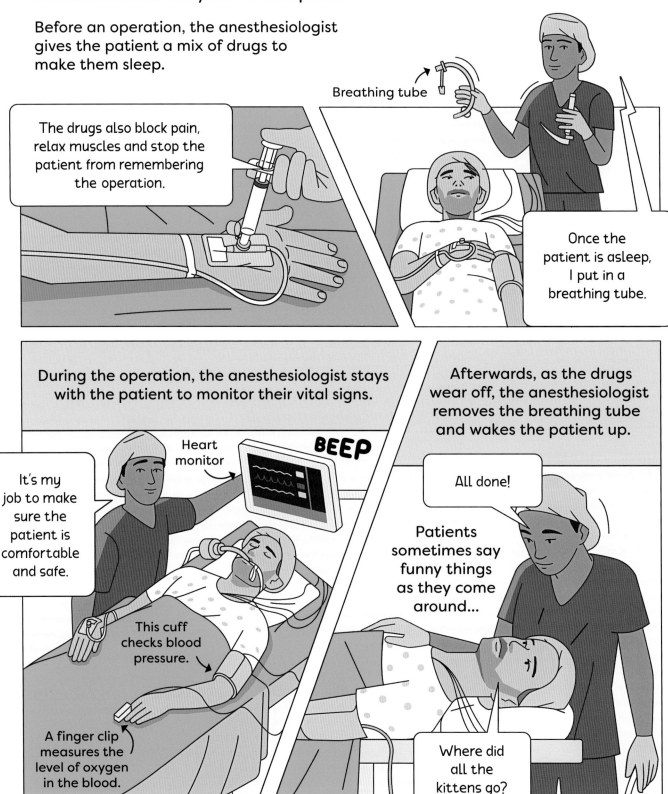

42

Blocking out pain

Sometimes, rather than sending someone to sleep, anesthesiologists can numb just one part.

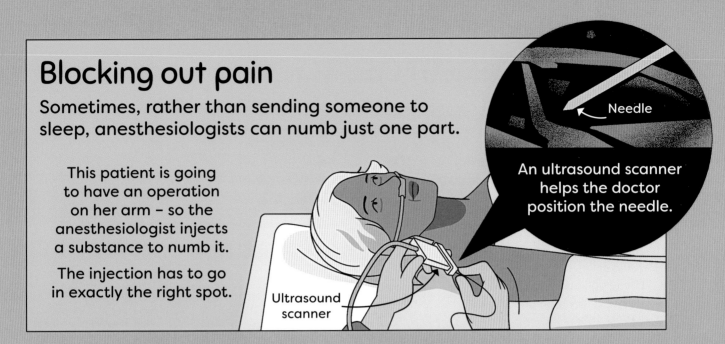

This patient is going to have an operation on her arm – so the anesthesiologist injects a substance to numb it.

The injection has to go in exactly the right spot.

Ultrasound scanner

Needle

An ultrasound scanner helps the doctor position the needle.

Brain surgery

For brain surgery, patients are put to sleep then sometimes woken up again. This allows NEUROSURGEONS (brain surgeons) to test the patient's brain as they operate.

These neurosurgeons are operating while their patient plays the violin! This helps them avoid damaging the parts needed for violin playing.

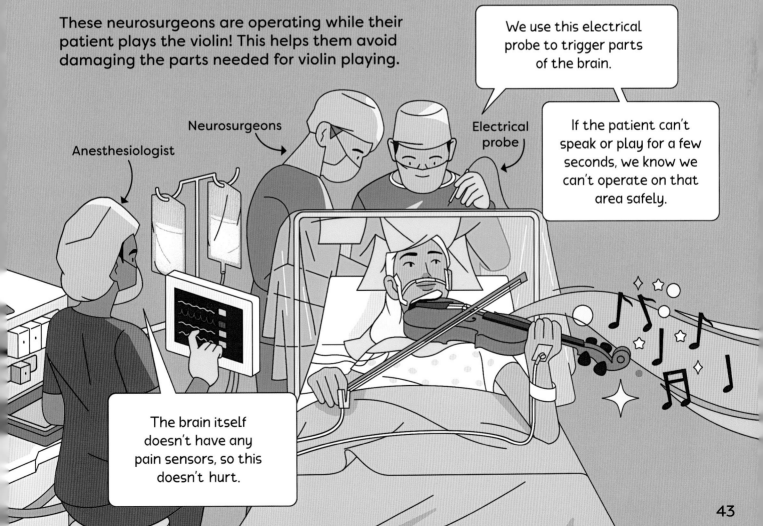

We use this electrical probe to trigger parts of the brain.

If the patient can't speak or play for a few seconds, we know we can't operate on that area safely.

Anesthesiologist

Neurosurgeons

Electrical probe

The brain itself doesn't have any pain sensors, so this doesn't hurt.

Extraordinary surgery

Some operations are especially complicated and risky. But if they work, they improve lives hugely – or even save them.

One of the most challenging operations is a heart transplant – when a patient with a failing heart receives a replacement. It's so difficult that it is only attempted when all other treatments have failed.

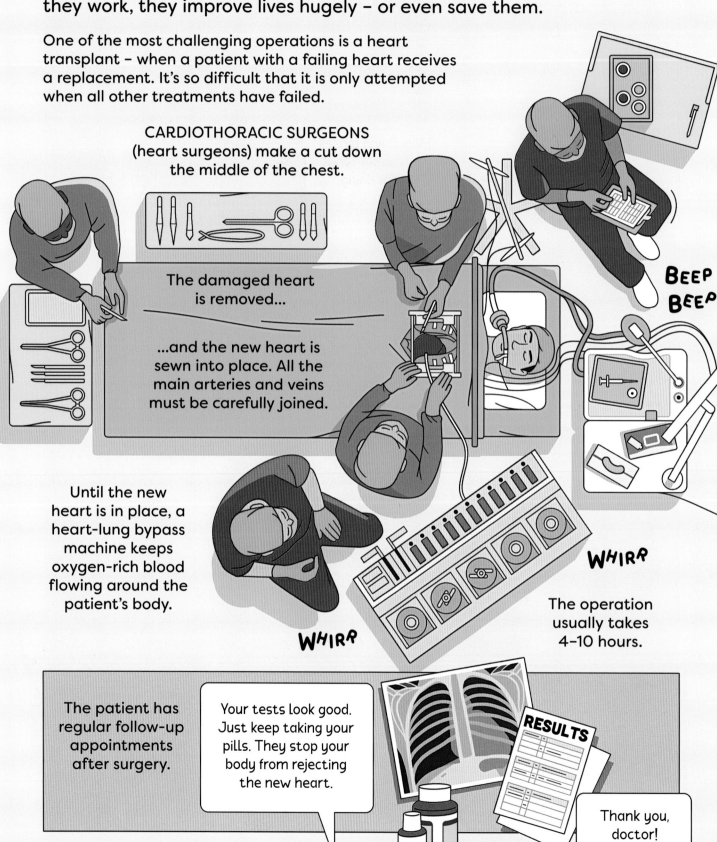

CARDIOTHORACIC SURGEONS (heart surgeons) make a cut down the middle of the chest.

The damaged heart is removed...

...and the new heart is sewn into place. All the main arteries and veins must be carefully joined.

BEEP BEEP

Until the new heart is in place, a heart-lung bypass machine keeps oxygen-rich blood flowing around the patient's body.

WHIRR

WHIRR

The operation usually takes 4–10 hours.

The patient has regular follow-up appointments after surgery.

Your tests look good. Just keep taking your pills. They stop your body from rejecting the new heart.

RESULTS

Thank you, doctor!

Delicate repair work

Sometimes an accident or disease can damage part of someone's face, changing how they look. Repairing this can be incredibly challenging. It's often done by PLASTIC SURGEONS.

These plastic surgeons are operating on a patient with cancer.

One surgeon removes a cancerous lump from the cheek.

Magnifying lenses help us see what we're doing.

The other removes some flesh and bone, known as a "flap," from the patient's hip. This will be used to rebuild the cheek.

It's a fiddly operation. The veins I need to sew together are thinner than a piece of spaghetti!

Veins

A four-day operation

One of the longest ever operations took place in 2001. Twenty doctors worked in shifts over four days to separate twins born joined at the head.

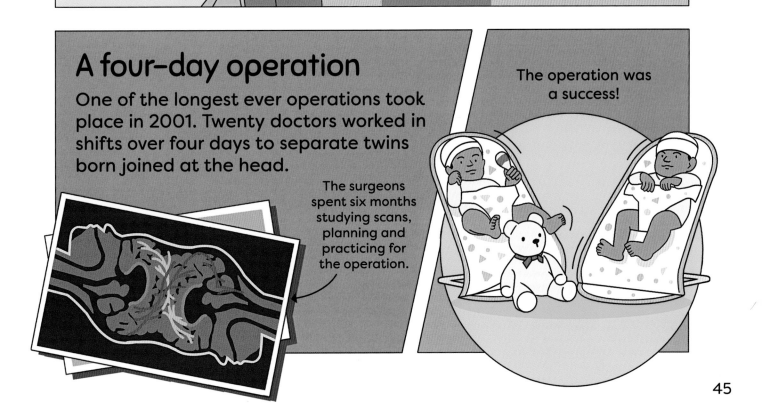

The surgeons spent six months studying scans, planning and practicing for the operation.

The operation was a success!

45

Keeping everyone healthy

The doctors below work to prevent disease, whether that's by checking blood pressure or fighting a pandemic.

PRIMARY CARE PHYSICIANS (PCPs) see patients in the community and are always on the lookout for early signs of disease.

INFECTIOUS DISEASE DOCTORS see patients with diseases that spread easily and can be dangerous.

PUBLIC HEALTH DOCTORS work to improve everyone's health – for example by rolling out vaccines or advising the government.

Keeping everyone healthy

Finding diseases early – or even stopping people from getting sick – is an important part of the job for some doctors. Many do this by seeing patients regularly, but others do it without seeing patients at all.

PEDIATRICIANS (children's doctors) and PRIMARY CARE PHYSICIANS (or family doctors) invite patients for check-ups at certain ages.

NEWBORN SCREENING

A pediatrician checks for common problems with eyes, heart and hips soon after birth.

> Your baby looks very healthy.

A COUPLE OF MONTHS OLD

A doctor examines the baby and checks growth is on track.

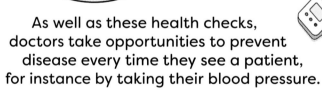

> She's growing well.

MIDDLE AGE

A doctor assesses the patient's risk of developing heart disease, diabetes, kidney disease or having a stroke.

As well as these health checks, doctors take opportunities to prevent disease every time they see a patient, for instance by taking their blood pressure.

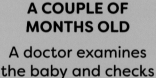

OLD AGE

Older patients should have more frequent check-ups.

> Finding a disease at an early stage makes it much easier to treat.

> Your blood pressure's high, which increases your risk of heart disease and strokes. I'll prescribe something to lower it.

PUBLIC HEALTH DOCTORS improve people's health by working with scientists and politicians.

An important part of this is vaccine programs. **Vaccines** are *preventative* medicines. They stop people from catching infectious diseases, such as measles or the flu.

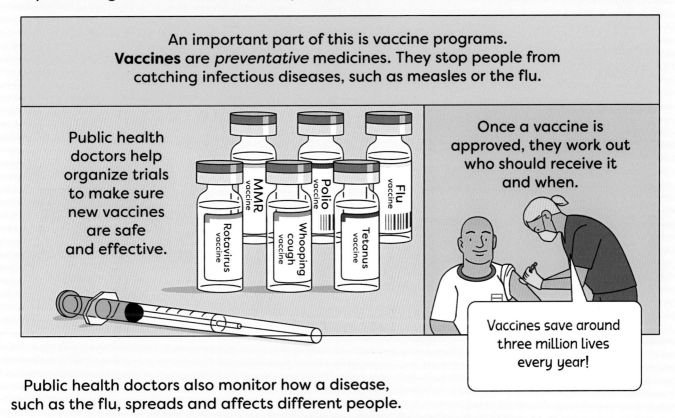

Public health doctors help organize trials to make sure new vaccines are safe and effective.

Once a vaccine is approved, they work out who should receive it and when.

Vaccines save around three million lives every year!

Public health doctors also monitor how a disease, such as the flu, spreads and affects different people.

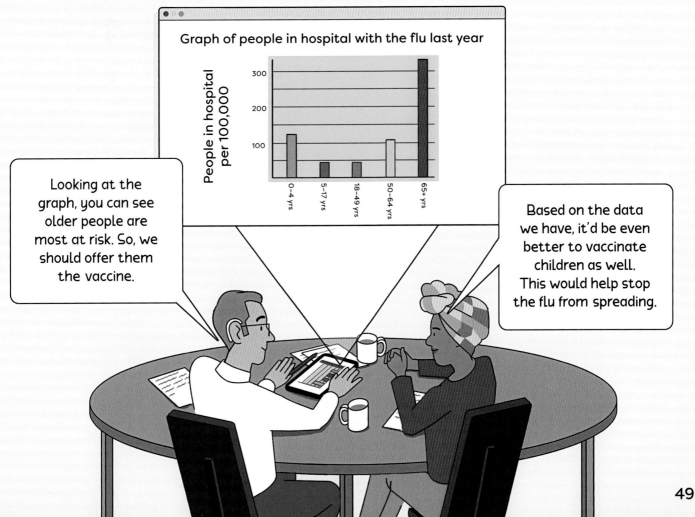

Graph of people in hospital with the flu last year

People in hospital per 100,000

300
200
100

0–4 yrs
5–17 yrs
18–49 yrs
50–64 yrs
65+ yrs

Looking at the graph, you can see older people are most at risk. So, we should offer them the vaccine.

Based on the data we have, it'd be even better to vaccinate children as well. This would help stop the flu from spreading.

Infectious diseases

Infectious diseases can spread quickly from one person to another, making lots of people unwell at the same time. So, doctors need to work together to keep any outbreaks under control.

The most serious diseases are **notifiable**. That means doctors have to report any cases.

We've just had a patient with bacterial meningitis.

A public health doctor decides what needs doing.

Please trace everyone they've spent time with, so we can treat them too.

Sewage is an important source of information for public health. The germs which cause disease often show up in poop – so testing sewage can give doctors an early warning.

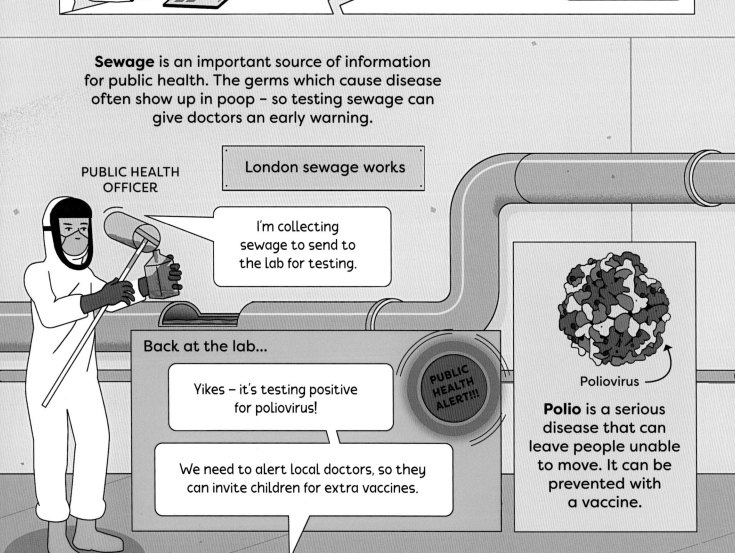

PUBLIC HEALTH OFFICER

London sewage works

I'm collecting sewage to send to the lab for testing.

Back at the lab...

Yikes – it's testing positive for poliovirus!

We need to alert local doctors, so they can invite children for extra vaccines.

PUBLIC HEALTH ALERT!!!

Poliovirus

Polio is a serious disease that can leave people unable to move. It can be prevented with a vaccine.

Dangerous and deadly

INFECTIOUS DISEASE DOCTOR is not a job for the faint-hearted. Some of these doctors work with the world's deadliest infectious diseases.

Infectious disease doctors have to take special precautions. To treat a patient safely, they may need to use a **High Level Isolation Unit** – a sealed, see-through tent with a bed inside.

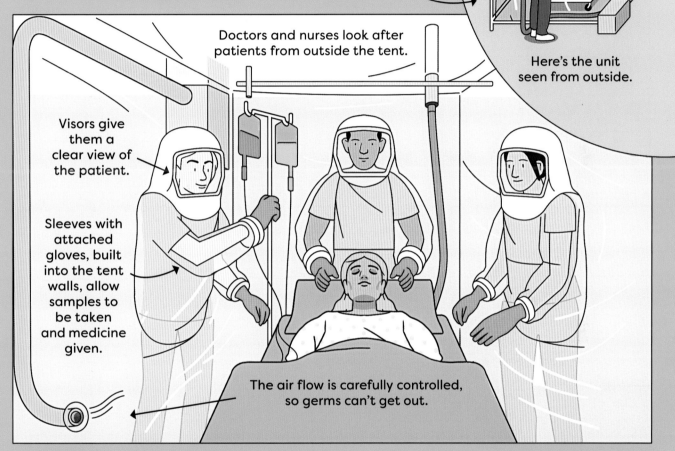

Here's the unit seen from outside.

Doctors and nurses look after patients from outside the tent.

Visors give them a clear view of the patient.

Sleeves with attached gloves, built into the tent walls, allow samples to be taken and medicine given.

The air flow is carefully controlled, so germs can't get out.

Infectious disease doctors do lab work too.

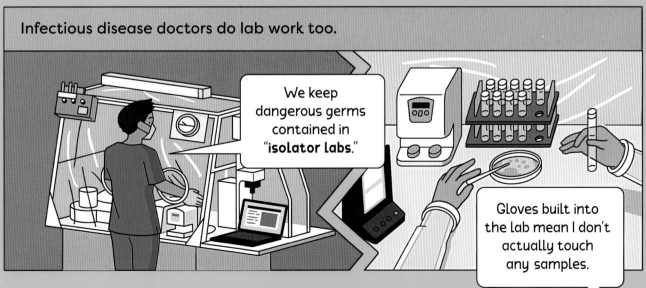

We keep dangerous germs contained in "isolator labs."

Gloves built into the lab mean I don't actually touch any samples.

Pandemic

If an outbreak becomes widespread, crossing into different countries, it's known as a **pandemic**. When this happens, doctors everywhere have to pull together and work incredibly hard.

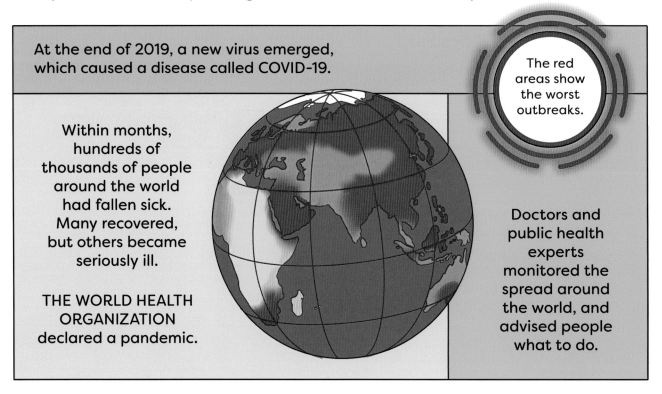

At the end of 2019, a new virus emerged, which caused a disease called COVID-19.

Within months, hundreds of thousands of people around the world had fallen sick. Many recovered, but others became seriously ill.

THE WORLD HEALTH ORGANIZATION declared a pandemic.

The red areas show the worst outbreaks.

Doctors and public health experts monitored the spread around the world, and advised people what to do.

Doctors and nurses cared for the sick. They wore special protective gear to try to avoid infection.

Taking it off is the trickiest part – any mistake exposes you to the virus.

Senior public health doctors gave advice to governments and people about what to do.

CHIEF MEDICAL OFFICER

NEWS BREAKING

Stay at home to stop the virus spreading.

Meanwhile, public health and infectious disease doctors worked with scientists to find out more about the virus and how it was making people sick.

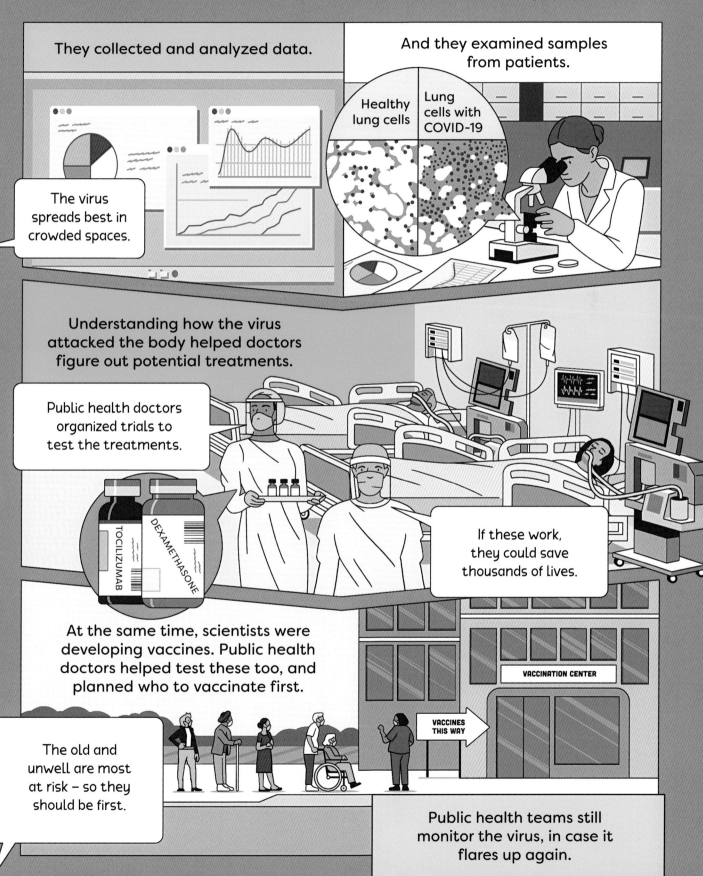

Fascinating brains

Some doctors specialize in treating the brain. Others are mental health experts, who help with conditions that affect people's thoughts and behavior.

NEUROLOGISTS diagnose and treat conditions affecting the brain and nervous system – the nerves that carry messages between brain and body.

NEUROSURGEONS perform surgery on the brain and nervous system.

PSYCHIATRISTS help people struggling with difficult thoughts and feelings.

Brain trouble

The brain is the body's most complicated organ. This makes it an especially challenging – and fascinating – area to work on. Brain doctors, called NEUROLOGISTS, are learning more about how the brain works all the time.

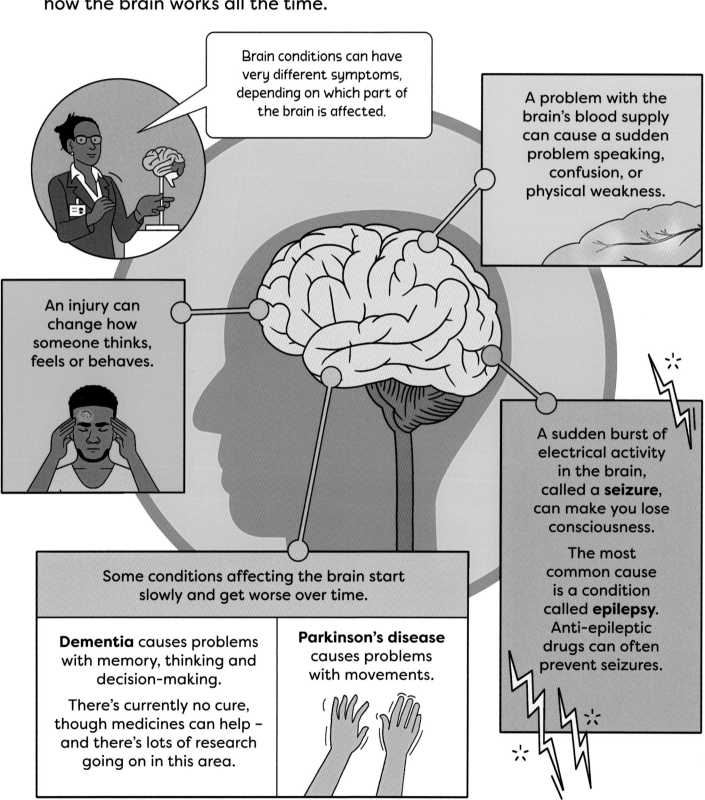

Brain conditions can have very different symptoms, depending on which part of the brain is affected.

A problem with the brain's blood supply can cause a sudden problem speaking, confusion, or physical weakness.

An injury can change how someone thinks, feels or behaves.

A sudden burst of electrical activity in the brain, called a **seizure**, can make you lose consciousness.

The most common cause is a condition called **epilepsy**. Anti-epileptic drugs can often prevent seizures.

Some conditions affecting the brain start slowly and get worse over time.

Dementia causes problems with memory, thinking and decision-making.

There's currently no cure, though medicines can help – and there's lots of research going on in this area.

Parkinson's disease causes problems with movements.

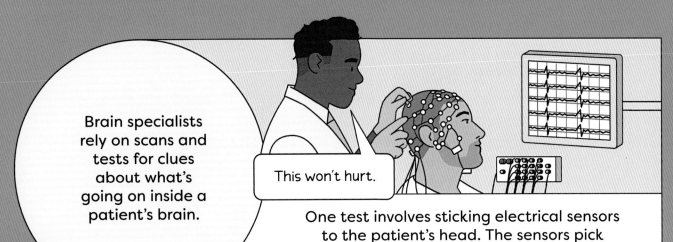

Brain specialists rely on scans and tests for clues about what's going on inside a patient's brain.

This won't hurt.

One test involves sticking electrical sensors to the patient's head. The sensors pick up electrical activity in the brain, which can help show if the patient has epilepsy.

Some brain conditions can be improved or cured with surgery. These tricky operations are carried out by NEUROSURGEONS (brain surgeons).

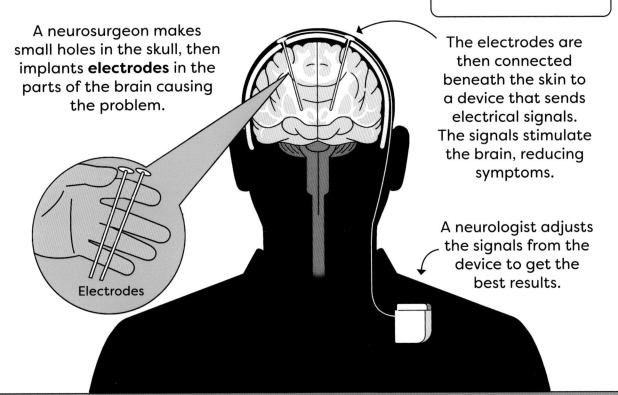

Deep brain stimulation is a treatment that can help with extreme stiffness or shakiness – such as that caused by Parkinson's disease.

We operate slowly and carefully so we don't damage important parts of the brain.

A neurosurgeon makes small holes in the skull, then implants **electrodes** in the parts of the brain causing the problem.

Electrodes

The electrodes are then connected beneath the skin to a device that sends electrical signals. The signals stimulate the brain, reducing symptoms.

A neurologist adjusts the signals from the device to get the best results.

Mysteries of the brain

There's a great deal that isn't understood about the brain and the problems that affect it. But research neurologists are working hard to unravel its mysteries. Here is just some of the work being done.

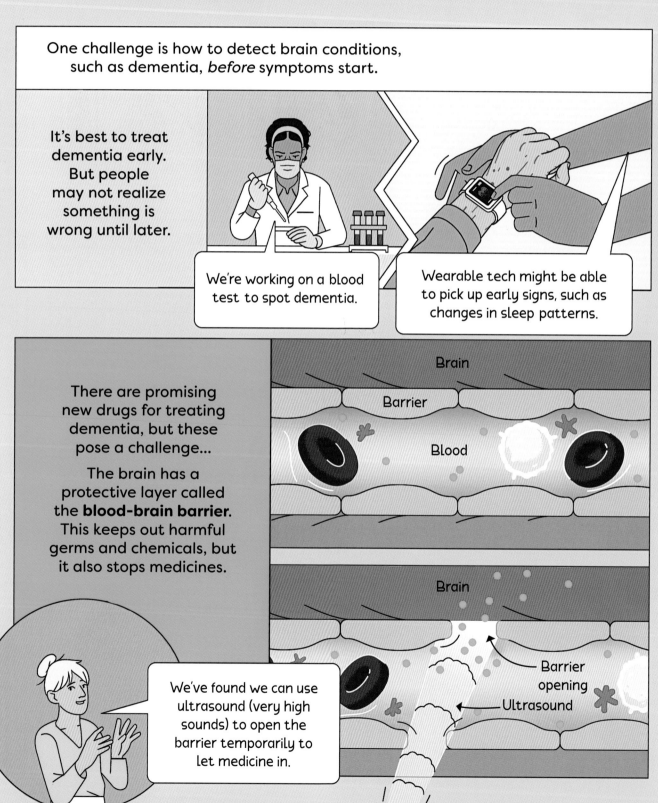

One challenge is how to detect brain conditions, such as dementia, *before* symptoms start.

It's best to treat dementia early. But people may not realize something is wrong until later.

We're working on a blood test to spot dementia.

Wearable tech might be able to pick up early signs, such as changes in sleep patterns.

There are promising new drugs for treating dementia, but these pose a challenge...

The brain has a protective layer called the **blood-brain barrier**. This keeps out harmful germs and chemicals, but it also stops medicines.

Brain

Barrier

Blood

Brain

Barrier opening

Ultrasound

We've found we can use ultrasound (very high sounds) to open the barrier temporarily to let medicine in.

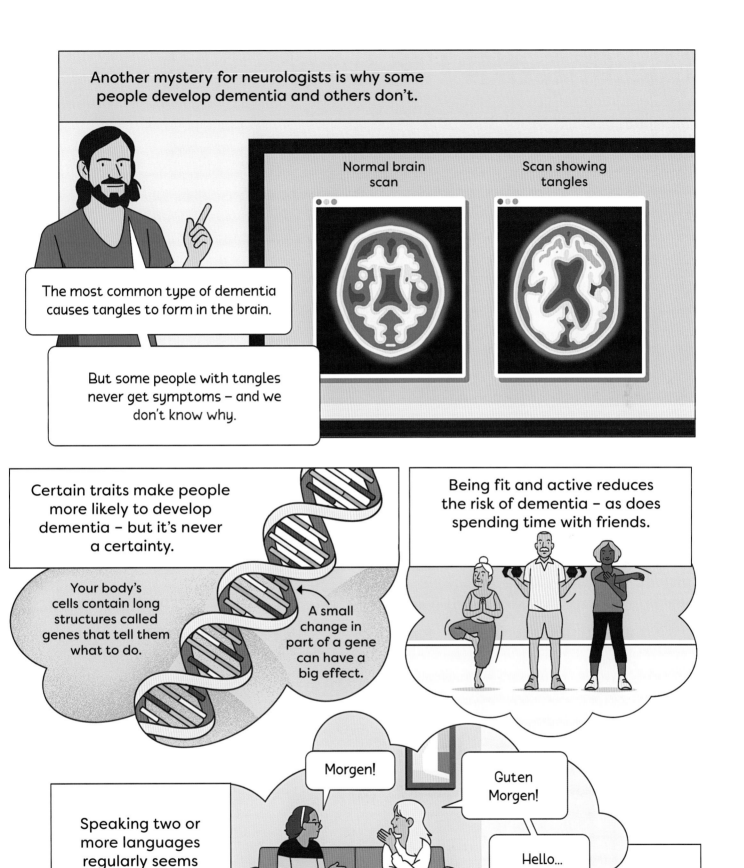

Looking after mental health

Minds can get unwell, just like bodies – and when they do, doctors are there to help. For these doctors, being a good listener is an especially important skill.

Primary care physicians are usually the first doctors people see when they're worried about how they're feeling.

A first appointment is generally followed by regular follow-up appointments, to check how things are going.

How are you? Has the medication helped?

Yes, I've been a lot less anxious.

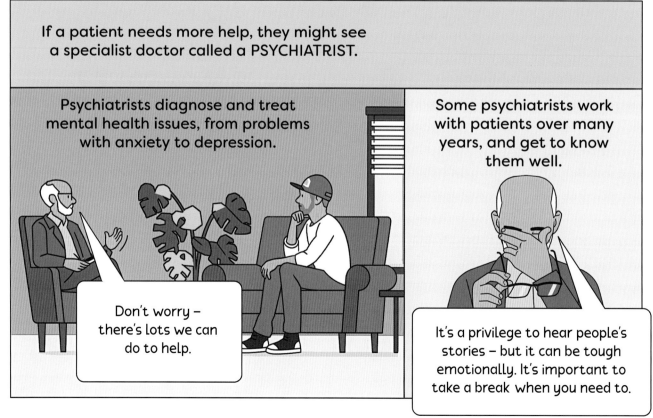

If a patient needs more help, they might see a specialist doctor called a PSYCHIATRIST.

Psychiatrists diagnose and treat mental health issues, from problems with anxiety to depression.

Some psychiatrists work with patients over many years, and get to know them well.

Don't worry – there's lots we can do to help.

It's a privilege to hear people's stories – but it can be tough emotionally. It's important to take a break when you need to.

Psychiatrists treat patients with medicines and talking therapies. Primary care physicians might prescribe medicines to help, send patients to see other professionals or suggest activities to try.

MUSIC THERAPISTS

Making and listening to music can help people communicate how they feel.

PSYCHOTHERAPISTS and COUNSELORS

We listen to patients and help them explore their thoughts and feelings.

CHILD PSYCHOLOGISTS

We help children understand and express their feelings through play.

BEREAVEMENT COUNSELORS

I help people after someone has died. We talk about grief and how they're coping.

COMMUNITY GROUPS

It feels good to connect with others.

EXERCISE CLASSES or CLUBS

Painting makes me feel much better.

The future of medicine

Medicine is changing all the time – and new discoveries can save countless lives. Here are some areas where new research is going on.

ONCOLOGISTS, or cancer specialists, are often involved in research or testing new treatments.

CLINICAL GENETICISTS are experts in genes – the instructions that control your body's cells – and the problems caused when genes go wrong.

RADIOLOGISTS are doctors who interpret scans to see what might be wrong.

PEDIATRIC SURGEONS perform operations on children and babies.

Fighting cancer

One of the fastest changing areas of medicine is cancer care. Doctors and scientists around the world are constantly working to develop new treatments.

Chemotherapy uses powerful chemicals to destroy cancers. Once it was an experimental, last-resort treatment, but ONCOLOGIST Dr. Jane C. Wright changed that...

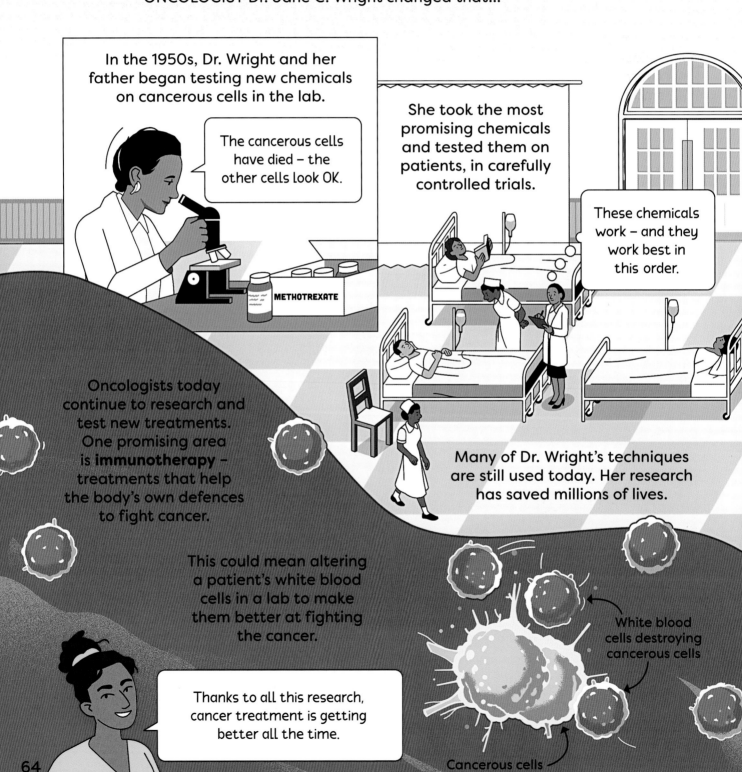

In the 1950s, Dr. Wright and her father began testing new chemicals on cancerous cells in the lab.

The cancerous cells have died – the other cells look OK.

METHOTREXATE

She took the most promising chemicals and tested them on patients, in carefully controlled trials.

These chemicals work – and they work best in this order.

Oncologists today continue to research and test new treatments. One promising area is **immunotherapy** – treatments that help the body's own defences to fight cancer.

Many of Dr. Wright's techniques are still used today. Her research has saved millions of lives.

This could mean altering a patient's white blood cells in a lab to make them better at fighting the cancer.

White blood cells destroying cancerous cells

Thanks to all this research, cancer treatment is getting better all the time.

Cancerous cells

Evolving roles

Technology is transforming some areas of medicine – for instance, working with genes.

Gene sequencing machine

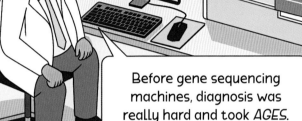

Finding and treating genetic problems means looking closely at the genes themselves. They're so small and complicated that this used to be very difficult.

CLINICAL GENETICIST

Before gene sequencing machines, diagnosis was really hard and took *AGES*.

Now we can test lots of genes at once and find the problem quickly.

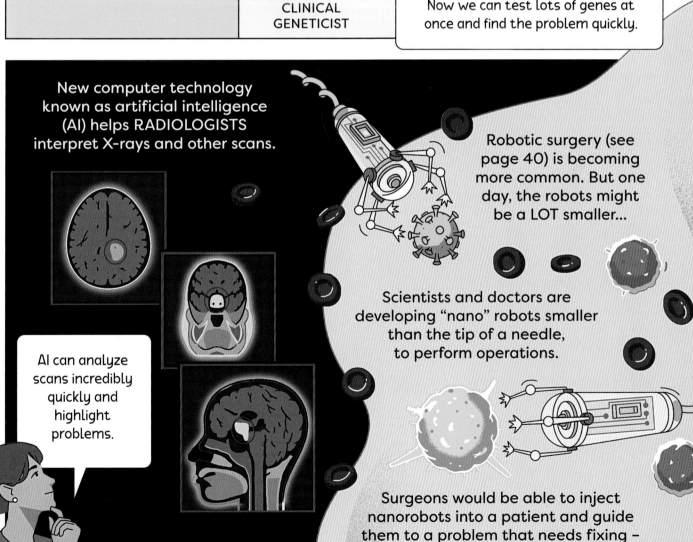

New computer technology known as artificial intelligence (AI) helps RADIOLOGISTS interpret X-rays and other scans.

AI can analyze scans incredibly quickly and highlight problems.

Robotic surgery (see page 40) is becoming more common. But one day, the robots might be a LOT smaller...

Scientists and doctors are developing "nano" robots smaller than the tip of a needle, to perform operations.

Surgeons would be able to inject nanorobots into a patient and guide them to a problem that needs fixing – all without making any cuts.

Learning and sharing knowledge

No matter how many qualifications doctors have, they need to keep their skills sharp and stay up-to-date. That means...

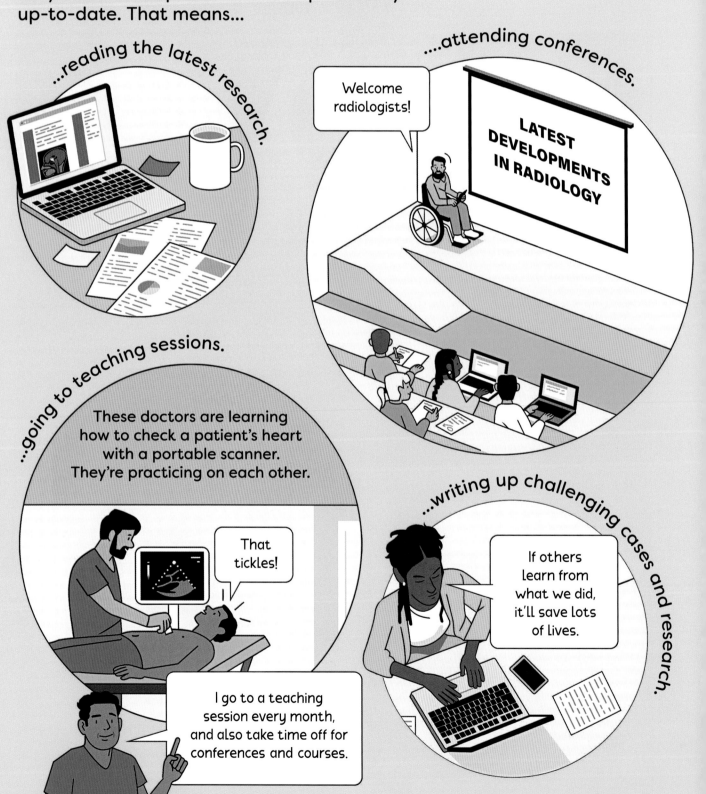

...reading the latest research.

....attending conferences.

Welcome radiologists!

LATEST DEVELOPMENTS IN RADIOLOGY

...going to teaching sessions.

These doctors are learning how to check a patient's heart with a portable scanner. They're practicing on each other.

That tickles!

I go to a teaching session every month, and also take time off for conferences and courses.

...writing up challenging cases and research.

If others learn from what we did, it'll save lots of lives.

Extraordinary new techniques

Sometimes, doctors travel abroad to learn or teach a new treatment.

In 2018, PEDIATRIC SURGEONS from the UK learned a pioneering technique for treating a condition called **spina bifida** from surgeons in Belgium and America.

Spina bifida is when a baby's spine doesn't form properly. This can lead to injuries to the brain and spinal cord, leaving the child unable to walk when they grow up.

Doctors can see spina bifida on an ultrasound scan before a baby is born.

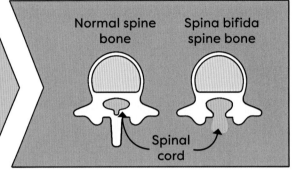

Normal spine bone

Spina bifida spine bone

Spinal cord

Surgeons operate to repair spina bifida and prevent further injuries. Usually this is done soon after birth. But the new operation can be done *before* birth.

The surgeons make a cut to reach the uterus (womb), where the baby is growing.

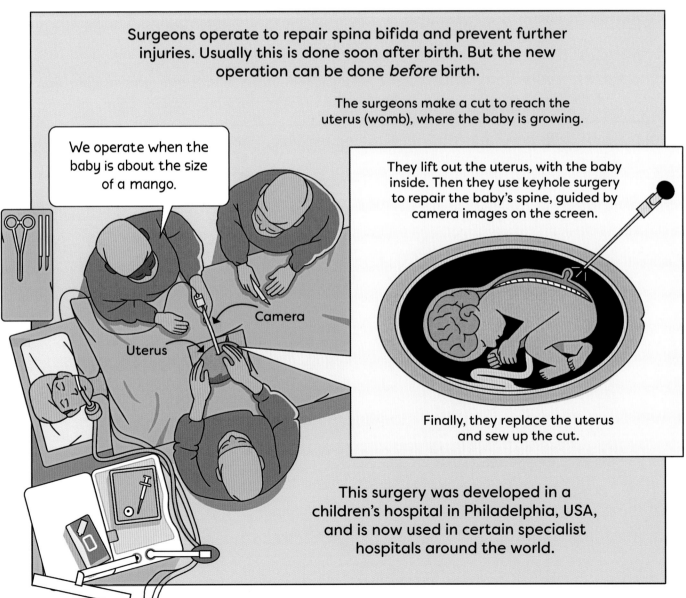

We operate when the baby is about the size of a mango.

Camera

Uterus

They lift out the uterus, with the baby inside. Then they use keyhole surgery to repair the baby's spine, guided by camera images on the screen.

Finally, they replace the uterus and sew up the cut.

This surgery was developed in a children's hospital in Philadelphia, USA, and is now used in certain specialist hospitals around the world.

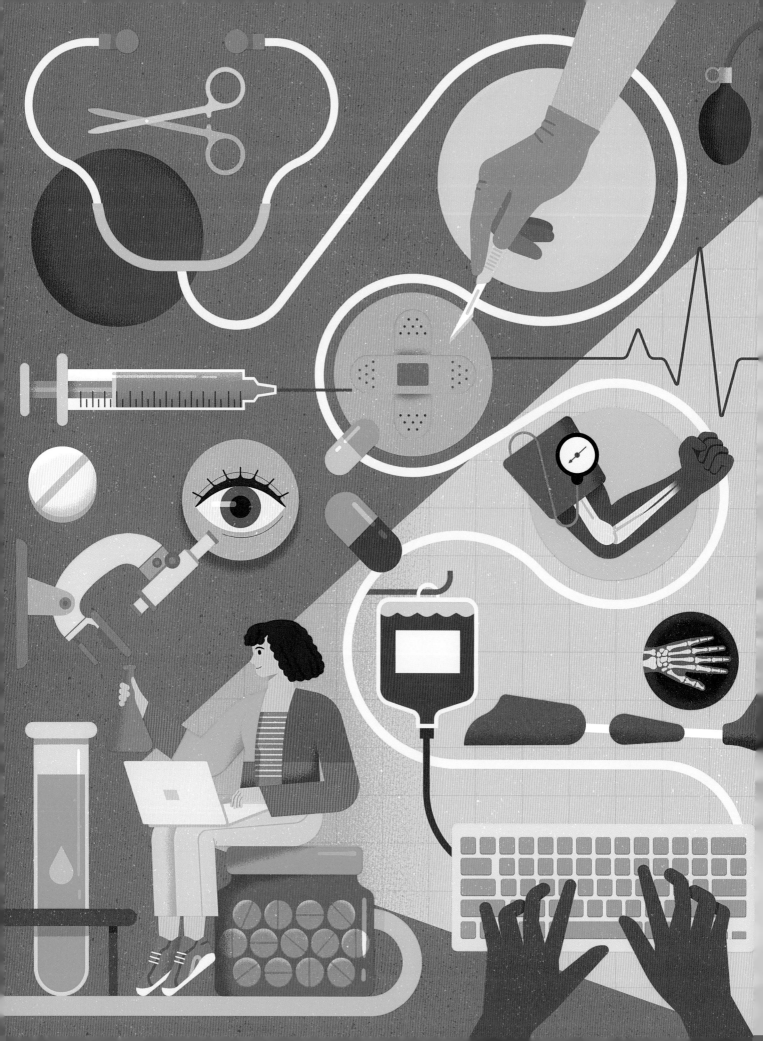

How to become a doctor

It typically takes at least ten years to finish training as one of the doctors in this book. But where do you begin?

Learn as much about the body and medicine as you can. You could read books, visit science museums or watch videos and TV shows.

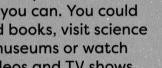

You'll need to take science classes at school, then go to medical school (university for doctors) for at least four years. And after that, there are years of training on the job.

Playing sports can teach you a lot about how to use your body and how to avoid injuries. And team sports will help you develop good communication and teamwork – important skills for doctors.

Being a doctor is also about helping others. Volunteering or raising money for charity can be a great way to start thinking about this and to build useful skills.

Curious about the human body and what it takes to be a doctor? Explore online for more information, videos and activities.

Scan the code for links to exciting websites, or visit **usborne.com/Quicklinks**

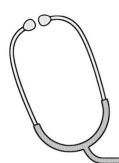

What happens in medical school?

Medical students find out all about how the body works – and not just from books...

> Today we're going to be dissecting a corpse, so you can see inside a real body.

Students also learn about all the things that can go wrong with the body.

Sometimes they develop "**Medical Student Syndrome.**" That's when they convince themselves they have all the horrible diseases they're studying.

> Am I having a heart attack?

> Is that tingling in my toes gangrene?

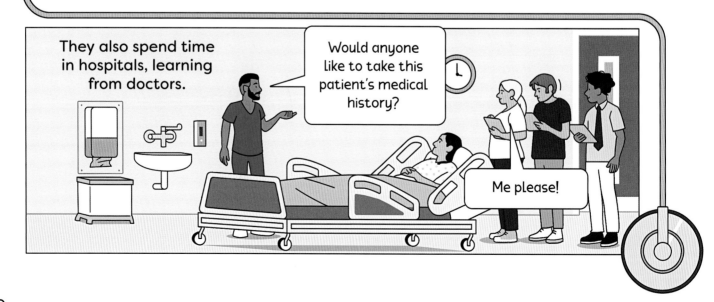

They also spend time in hospitals, learning from doctors.

> Would anyone like to take this patient's medical history?

> Me please!

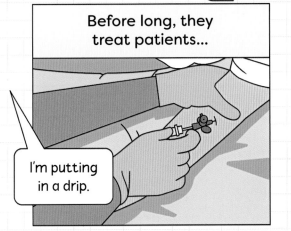

Before long, they treat patients...

I'm putting in a drip.

...and show more junior medical students what to do.

You learn by doing – it's very hands-on!

There are other **medical jobs** to consider, if you're not sure being a doctor is for you:

NURSES

provide more hands-on care than doctors. There are almost as many types of nurses as doctors.

PARAMEDICS

are trained to provide urgent, on-the-spot treatment. They often arrive first at the scene by ambulance.

NURSE MIDWIVES

help during pregnancy and childbirth, with support from a doctor if needed.

PHYSIOTHERAPISTS

help with exercise and recovery. They are very knowledgeable about bones and muscles.

PHARMACISTS

are specialists in preparing medicines. They can also diagnose minor problems.

Anatomy

Medical students have to know the body inside out. Learning about all the different parts and how they fit together is called **anatomy**.

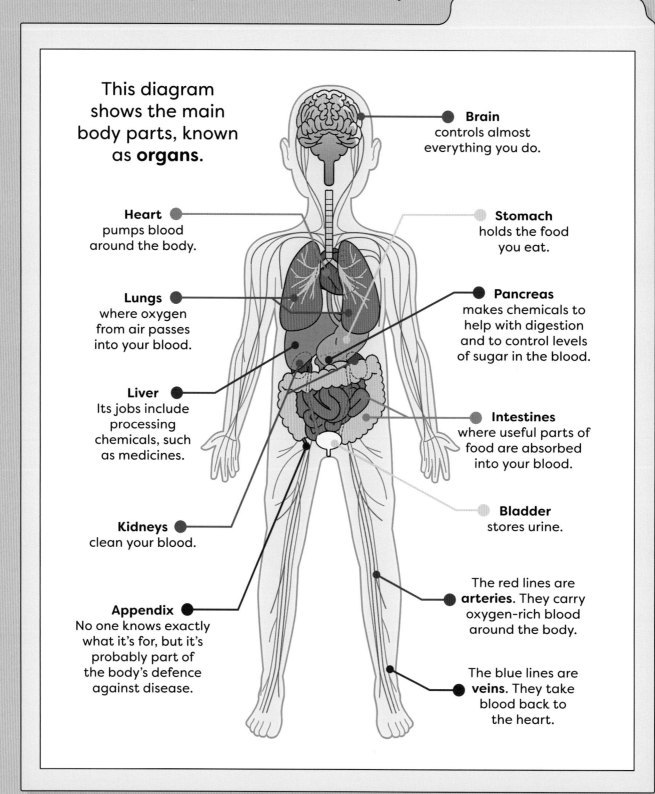

This diagram shows the main body parts, known as **organs**.

Brain
controls almost everything you do.

Heart
pumps blood around the body.

Stomach
holds the food you eat.

Lungs
where oxygen from air passes into your blood.

Pancreas
makes chemicals to help with digestion and to control levels of sugar in the blood.

Liver
Its jobs include processing chemicals, such as medicines.

Intestines
where useful parts of food are absorbed into your blood.

Kidneys
clean your blood.

Bladder
stores urine.

The red lines are **arteries**. They carry oxygen-rich blood around the body.

Appendix
No one knows exactly what it's for, but it's probably part of the body's defence against disease.

The blue lines are **veins**. They take blood back to the heart.

The human body has more than two hundred bones – each with its own Latin name, which medical students have to memorize.

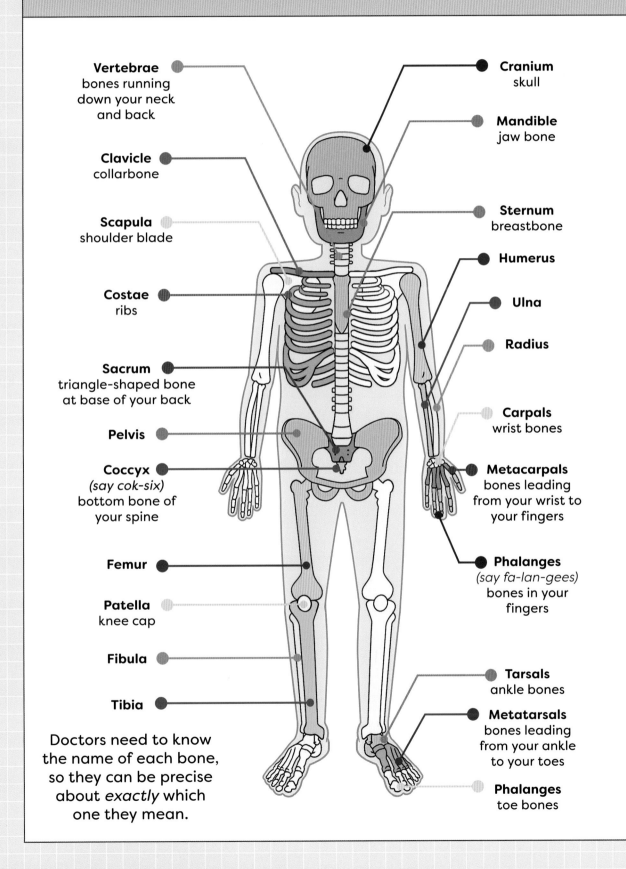

Vertebrae
bones running down your neck and back

Clavicle
collarbone

Scapula
shoulder blade

Costae
ribs

Sacrum
triangle-shaped bone at base of your back

Pelvis

Coccyx
(say cok-six)
bottom bone of your spine

Femur

Patella
knee cap

Fibula

Tibia

Cranium
skull

Mandible
jaw bone

Sternum
breastbone

Humerus

Ulna

Radius

Carpals
wrist bones

Metacarpals
bones leading from your wrist to your fingers

Phalanges
(say fa-lan-gees)
bones in your fingers

Tarsals
ankle bones

Metatarsals
bones leading from your ankle to your toes

Phalanges
toe bones

Doctors need to know the name of each bone, so they can be precise about *exactly* which one they mean.

Which job?

If you think you'd like to be a doctor, answer these questions to find out which sort might be right for you.

Which of these describes you best?

You're not at all squeamish, and you're good at working with your hands.

You'd like to carry out research and use cutting-edge techniques and treatments.

You want to make people happier and healthier.

You want to work somewhere that's fast-paced, with lots of drama.

Which would you most enjoy...

...looking after the very sickest patients?

...life-saving emergency work?

...working with mothers and babies?

You could become an **ICU doctor.**

You might enjoy being an **ER doctor**, **air ambulance doctor** or **humanitarian doctor.**

You might make a good **obstetrician** or **neonatologist.**

Would you most like...

...doing intricate, fiddly operations? → You might be a great **plastic surgeon** or **otolaryngologist** (an **ear, nose and throat physician**).

...to perform dramatic, life-saving surgery? → You could be a **cardiothoracic surgeon**.

...using technology to assist with operations? → You might enjoy robotic surgery. Lots of surgeons use this technique, including **general surgeons**.

You're most interested in...

...new technology and gadgets. →

...developing and using new cancer treatments. → You could be an **oncologist**.

...deciphering the mysteries of the brain. → You might enjoy being a **neurologist**.

Would you most enjoy...

...planning how best to test new medicines and who to vaccinate when? → You might make a great **public health doctor**.

...listening to patients and helping them with all kinds of medical problems? → You might enjoy working as a **primary care physician**, or as a **psychiatrist**.

Medical terms

Here are some of the medical terms
used in this book.

appendicitis – when an organ in your belly, called the appendix, is swollen. It often makes the lower right side of your belly very sore.

bacteria – tiny living things. Some are **germs**.

cancer – a condition where **cells** in part of the body grow uncontrollably. There are lots of different types.

cells – the tiny building blocks that make up every part of your body. There are lots of different types, such as **red blood cells** and **white blood cells** in your blood.

chemotherapy – a treatment that uses powerful chemicals to destroy **cancer**.

consultation – the name for a patient–doctor meeting.

COVID-19 – an infectious disease caused by a **virus**. It emerged at the end of 2019 and led to a **pandemic**.

CT (computed tomography) scans – detailed slice-by-slice images of the body made using X-rays and assembled by a computer.

dementia – the name for a group of conditions that cause problems with memory, thinking and decision-making.

deep brain stimulation – a treatment where parts of the brain causing problems are stimulated with electrical pulses. It can help with extreme stiffness or shakiness – such as that caused by Parkinson's disease.

diagnosing – working out what problem a patient has by looking at their symptoms.

genes – a set of instructions inside a **cell** that tells it what to do. When genes go wrong, it can cause problems such as **cancer**.

germs - microscopic things, such as **bacteria** and **viruses**, that make you sick by invading your body. Doctors know of around 1,400 germs that can make humans sick.

heart attack – a serious problem caused when the supply of blood to the heart is blocked.

immunotherapy – a treatment that uses the body's own defences to fight **cancer**.

incubator – an enclosed bed with temperature controls to help keep a very sick or small baby comfortable.

infectious – the word for when a disease spreads easily from person to person. Infectious diseases are caused by **germs**.

medical history – all of a patient's past medical problems and treatments.

medical school – a university department where students study medicine in order to become doctors.

MRI (magnetic resonance imaging) scans – detailed slice-by-slice images of the body made by a scanner using strong magnets.

nerves – long, thin fibers that carry messages between the brain and body. They're how you know if something you're touching is hot or cold, fluffy or sharp.

nervous system – the network of **nerves** that carry messages between your brain and your body.

norovirus – an **infectious virus** that causes vomiting.

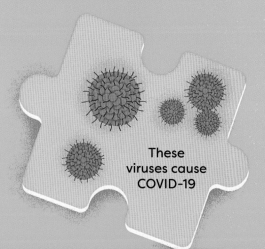

These viruses cause COVID-19

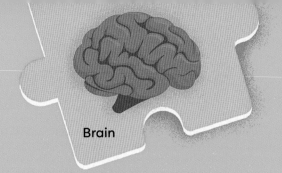

Brain

organ – a main body part, such as the heart, lungs or brain.

pandemic – when a disease spreads widely, crossing into different countries.

Parkinson's disease – a condition affecting the brain. It causes problems with movements and gradually gets worse over time.

petri dish – a round, flat dish doctors and scientists grow **bacteria** in.

physical examination – when a doctor looks at, feels or listens to part of someone's body.

polio – a serious disease that can leave people unable to move. It can be prevented with a vaccine.

red blood cells – red, disc-shaped **cells** in your blood. They carry oxygen.

samples – little bits of something from a patient – such as urine, or **cells** – taken to help doctors make a diagnosis.

scans – images that show doctors inside the body. There are lots of different types, including **CT**, **MRI**, **ultrasound** and **X-ray** scans.

seizure – a burst of uncontrolled electrical activity in the brain. It can make someone move or behave in strange ways, or lose consciousness.

shingles – a disease caused by a **virus**. The same virus also causes chicken pox.

spina bifida – a condition where a baby's spine doesn't form properly, leaving the brain and spinal cord at risk of damage.

stroke – a problem with the blood supply to the brain. It can cause sudden difficulty speaking, confusion, or physical weakness.

taking a (medical) history – finding out about a patient's past and present medical problems.

ultrasound scans – images of inside the body made using ultrasound (sounds too high to hear).

viruses – the smallest kinds of **germ**.

vital signs – basic measurements doctors take to assess your health.

white blood cells – **cells** found in your blood. They are part of the body's defence against disease.

X-ray scans – images of inside the body made using X-rays – powerful waves of energy that you can't see.

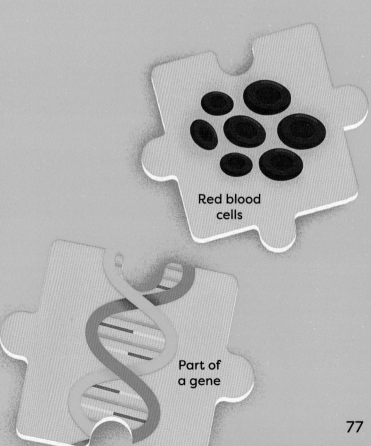

Red blood cells

Part of a gene

Jobs in medicine

Here are all of the different types of doctors mentioned in this book.
You can look them up in the index to find out which pages they're on.

AIR AMBULANCE DOCTORS fly out to give urgent emergency care to patients on the spot.

ANESTHESIOLOGISTS put patients to sleep before operations so they can't feel anything, and monitor them while surgeons work.

CARDIOTHORACIC SURGEONS operate on hearts and lungs.

CLINICAL GENETICISTS are experts in genes – the instructions that control your body's cells – and the problems caused when genes go wrong.

DERMATOLOGISTS diagnose and treat skin problems.

ER (EMERGENCY ROOM) DOCTORS treat people with injuries and emergency medical conditions when they arrive at the hospital.

EXPEDITION DOCTORS work in extreme locations, dealing with whatever medical problems arise.

GENERAL SURGEONS do common operations, such as removing a swollen appendix (a minor organ), or repairing a hole in muscle, called a hernia.

GERIATRICIANS are experts in treating older people.

HEMATOLOGISTS are blood specialists, who diagnose and treat blood problems.

HUMANITARIAN DOCTORS help out when disaster strikes, anywhere in the world.

INFECTIOUS DISEASE DOCTORS see patients with diseases that spread easily and can be dangerous.

INTENSIVE CARE DOCTORS look after the sickest patients in hospital.

NEONATOLOGISTS are doctors who look after newborn babies, especially ones that are unwell or born early.

NEUROLOGISTS diagnose and treat conditions affecting the brain or nervous system – the nerves that carry messages between brain and body.

NEUROSURGEONS perform surgery on the brain and nervous system.

OBSTETRICIANS provide care during pregnancy and birth.

ONCOLOGISTS are cancer specialists, who often work with extraordinary new treatments.

ORTHOPEDIC SURGEONS repair broken bones and joints. They use saws and drills, so are sometimes jokingly called carpenters.

OTOLARYNGOLOGISTS operate on ears, noses and throats. Also known as ENTs.

PATHOLOGISTS work in labs, where they examine urine and other samples from patients for signs of disease.

PEDIATRICIANS are doctors who look after sick children.

PEDIATRIC SURGEONS perform challenging operations on children and babies.

PLASTIC SURGEONS restore appearance to body parts after disease or injury.

PRIMARY CARE PHYSICIANS (PCPs) are usually the first doctors you see when you feel sick. They work in a doctor's office, looking after people who live locally.

PSYCHIATRISTS treat patients who are struggling with difficult thoughts or feelings.

PUBLIC HEALTH DOCTORS work to improve everyone's health – for example by rolling out vaccines or advising governments.

RADIOLOGISTS are doctors who interpret X-rays and other images showing inside the body, to see what might be wrong.

There are even more types of doctors than listed here, and almost as many nurse specialties. Visit **usborne.com/Quicklinks** and type in the title of this book to find out about some of these, plus other medical careers.

Index

A

air ambulance doctors, 27, 32–33, 74, 78
anatomy, 72–73
anesthesiologists, 25, 37, 39, 42–43, 78

B

babies, 12, 24–25, 48, 67, 74
bacteria, 50, 76
blood, 10, 14, 29, 32, 44, 56, 58, 72
    pressure, 10, 42, 48
blood-brain barrier, 58
bones, 67, 73
brain, 12, 13, 29, 45, 55, 56–59, 67, 72

C

cancer, 15, 35, 45, 63, 64, 76
cardiothoracic surgeon, 37, 44, 75, 78
cells, 14, 15, 64, 76
chemotherapy, 35, 64
clinical geneticists, 63, 65, 78
clinics, 18, 19, 22, 24
COVID-19, 52–53, 76
CT (computed tomography) scan, 13, 76

D

deep brain stimulation, 57, 76
dementia, 56, 58–59, 76
dermatologists, 17, 18, 78
diseases, 7, 34–35, 45, 47, 48–49, 50–51,
    52–53, 57, 70

E

ER (Emergency room), 27, 28–29, 74, 78
ER doctors, 26, 27–28, 74, 78
expedition doctors, 27, 35, 78

G

general surgeons, 37, 75, 78

genes, 59, 65, 76
geriatricians, 17, 19, 78
germs, 14, 38, 50–51, 58, 76

H

hematologists, 7, 14, 78
hospitals, 7, 17–25, 27–31
humanitarian doctors, 27, 34, 74, 78

I

inflatable hospitals, 34
intensive care doctors, 27, 30–31, 74, 78
intensive care unit (ICU), 27, 29, 30–31
infections, 10, 11, 12, 14, 38, 52
infectious diseases, 49, 50–51, 52–53, 76
infectious disease doctors, 47, 51, 53, 78

M

medical school, 69, 70–71, 76
medicines, 8, 14, 19, 30, 38, 49, 51, 56, 58,
    61, 64, 71
mental health, 9, 29, 55, 60–61
MRI (magnetic resonance imaging), 13,
    76–77

N

neonatologists, 17, 25, 74, 78
neurologists, 29, 55, 56–57, 58–59, 75, 78
neurosurgeons, 43, 55, 57, 78
nurse midwives, 24, 71
nurses, 19, 28, 30–31, 34, 38, 51, 52, 71, 78

O

obstetricians, 12, 17, 24–25, 74, 78
oncologists, 63, 64, 75, 78
operating theater, 34, 38–39
organs, 10, 56–57, 72, 77
orthopedic surgeons, 37, 38, 78
otolaryngologists, 37, 41, 75, 78

P

pediatricians, 17, 20–21, 48, 78
pediatric surgeons, 63, 67, 78
pager, 22–23
pandemics, 47, 52–53, 76
paramedics, 32–33, 71
Parkinson's disease, 56, 57, 77
pathologists, 7, 14–15, 78
pharmacists, 19, 71
plastic surgeons, 37, 45, 75, 78
primary care physicians (PCPs), 7, 8–9, 11, 47,
    48, 60, 75, 78
psychiatrists, 29, 55, 60–61, 75, 78
public health, 50, 52–53
public health doctors, 47, 49, 50, 52–53,
    75, 78

R

radiographers, 12
radiologists, 7, 12–13, 63, 65, 66, 78
red blood cells, 9, 14, 76, 77
resuscitation (resus), 29
robots, 40, 65, 75

S

scans, 12–13, 20, 29, 30, 43, 45, 57, 59, 63, 65,
    66–67, 77
sonographers, 12
surgeons, 37, 38–41, 43, 44–45, 67, 75
    cardiothoracic, 37, 44, 75, 78
    general, 37, 75, 78
    neurosurgeons, 43, 55, 57, 78
    orthopedic, 37, 38, 78
    pediatric, 63, 67, 78
    plastic, 37, 45, 75, 78
surgery, 23, 25, 32, 35, 37, 38–45, 55,
    57, 65, 67

T

tests, 9, 14, 18, 20–21, 44, 57, 58

U

ultrasound scans, 12, 30, 43, 67, 77

V

vaccines, 49, 50, 53
viruses, 8, 20, 50, 52–53, 66, 67
vital signs, 10, 42, 77

W

wards, 19, 20–21
    intensive care unit (ICU), 25,
        29, 30–31
    maternity ward, 24
    pediatric wad, 20–21
    prenatal ward, 24
ward rounds, 20–21
white blood cells, 14, 64, 77

X

X-ray scans, 7, 11, 12–13, 31,
    63, 77

Series designer: Zoe Wray   **Additional design: Jodie Smith**   **Series editor: Rosie Dickins**

First published in 2025 by Usborne Publishing Limited, 83-85 Saffron Hill, London EC1N 8RT, United Kingdom. usborne.com Copyright © 2025 Usborne Publishing Limited. The name Usborne and the Balloon logo are registered trade marks of Usborne Publishing Limited. All rights reserved. No part of this publication may be reproduced, stored in a retrieval system or transmitted in any form or by any means without prior permission of the publisher. AE. Printed in UAE. First published in America in 2025.

Usborne Publishing is not responsible and does not accept liability for the availability or content of any website other than its own, or for any exposure to harmful, offensive or inaccurate material which may appear on the Web. Usborne Publishing will have no liability for any damage or loss caused by viruses that may be downloaded as a result of browsing the sites it recommends.